What people are saying about …

THE FIRST FEW YEARS OF MARRIAGE

"Every couple needs a boost. Every couple deserves a great marriage. Jim and Doug are wonderful guides along the way."

John Ortberg, senior pastor of Menlo Church, author of *All the Places to Go*

"Drawing from Scripture, countless conversations with young couples, and lessons learned in their own long and successful marriages, Jim Burns and Doug Fields share the biblical principles that form the foundation of a happy and healthy relationship. If you want your marriage to go the distance, set the right tone early using the advice and practical application you'll find in this helpful book."

Jim Daly, president, Focus on the Family

"Great marriages are not born, they are developed. And like anything else in life, the sooner we work on improving matters, the better our results will be. Burns and Fields have created a unique, highly valuable and practical guide to those critical first years of the relationship. Highly recommended."

John Townsend, PhD, *New York Times* bestselling author of *Boundaries*, founder of the Townsend Institute for Leadership and Counseling, psychologist

"The book you hold in your hands is so important. Their advice is practical and doable. What you do in the first few years of your marriage, if you make wise decisions, will open the doorway to a successful marriage."

Gary Chapman, PhD, author
of *The 5 Love Languages*

"You've heard it said, 'How you finish is more important than how you start.' I disagree. How you start is very important and has much to do with how you finish. Don't wait until a crisis hits your marriage to seek wise counsel. The sooner you start the better. *The First Few Years of Marriage* by Jim Burns and Doug Fields is both wise counsel and a great start for your marriage."

Ted Cunningham, pastor, Woodland Hills
Family Church and author of *Fun Loving You*

"I wish this existed in 2001. It's so easy to make many mistakes right out of the gate. If you've just said 'I do,' pick this book up and save yourself a lot of trouble."

Jon Acuff, *New York Times*
bestselling author and speaker

"The early years of marriage play a huge role in whether or not what follows turns out to be a 'love' story, a 'roommates' story, or an 'at-least-we-didn't-get-divorced' story. If you're getting married or recently tied the knot, and would like to save yourselves a lot of unnecessary heartache, read this book."

Dr. Tim Kimmel, author of *Grace Filled Marriage*

"Jim and Doug have done it again! First, we made their book *Getting Ready for Marriage* part of our marriage strategy, and now this one will be added to it too. Excellent. Practical help. I'm excited to see how it will shape the next generation of marriages and put them on the right path. A must read for newly married couples ... heck, I've been married thirty years and I learned a lot too."

Reggie Joiner, founder of Orange

"I love my marriage. And I love Jim and Doug's book because it tackles the daily and deepest questions every marriage faces with authenticity, empathy, and wisdom."

Kara Powell, PhD, executive director of the Fuller
Youth Institute and coauthor of *Growing Young*

"We love this book! Jim and Doug are real, personal, and honest about the challenges they faced in the early years of their marriages and what they wish they had known that would have made things easier. Not only do they share how to surmount the challenges of the first years of marriage, but also how to have some fun along the way. So if you want to ensure that your marriage will thrive in the years ahead, take this book home and read it together—starting tonight."

Claudia and David Arp, MSW authors
of the 10 Great Dates® series

"If you want solid, time-tested wisdom about making marriage work, don't ask Google. Ask Jim and Doug. They have assembled the best research and practical wisdom of the ages with their years of counseling and real-life marriage experience to give you a manual for getting it right. When you start a new job, a how-to manual from those who have gone before you is helpful, right? This is your marriage manual to get started on a marriage that will last a lifetime."

Ron L. Deal, family trainer and therapist,
author of *The Smart Stepfamily Marriage*

THE
FIRST FEW YEARS
OF MARRIAGE

JIM BURNS & DOUG FIELDS

THE
FIRST FEW YEARS
OF MARRIAGE

8 WAYS TO STRENGTHEN YOUR "I DO"

David C Cook®

transforming lives together

THE FIRST FEW YEARS OF MARRIAGE
Published by David C Cook
4050 Lee Vance Drive
Colorado Springs, CO 80918 U.S.A.

David C Cook U.K., Kingsway Communications
Eastbourne, East Sussex BN23 6NT, England

The graphic circle C logo is a registered trademark of David C Cook.

The website addresses recommended throughout this book are offered as a
resource to you. These websites are not intended in any way to be or imply an
endorsement on the part of David C Cook, nor do we vouch for their content.

Details in some stories have been changed to protect the identities of the persons involved.

Unless otherwise noted, all Scripture quotations are taken from the Holy Bible, NEW
INTERNATIONAL VERSION®, NIV®. Copyright © 1973, 2011 by Biblica, Inc.® Used
by permission. All rights reserved worldwide. NEW INTERNATIONAL VERSION®
and NIV® are registered trademarks of Biblica, Inc. Use of either trademark for the
offering of goods or services requires the prior written consent of Biblica, Inc. Scripture
quotations marked ESV are taken from the ESV® Bible (The Holy Bible, English Standard
Version®), copyright © 2001 by Crossway, a publishing ministry of Good News Publishers.
Used by permission. All rights reserved; NLT are taken from the *Holy Bible*, New Living
Translation, copyright © 1996, 2007 by Tyndale House Foundation. Used by permission
of Tyndale House Publishers, Inc., Carol Stream, Illinois 60188. All rights reserved.
The author has added italics to Scripture quotations for emphasis.

LCCN 2017931012
ISBN 978-0-7814-1198-1
eISBN 978-1-4347-1109-0

The Authors are represented by and this book is published in association with the
literary agency of WordServe Literary Group, Ltd., www.wordserveliterary.com.

The Team: Tim Peterson, Keith Jones, Amy Konyndyk, Nick Lee,
Abby DeBenedittis, Stephanie Bennett, Susan Murdock
Cover Design: Nick Lee
Cover Photo: Getty Images

Printed in the United States of America
First Edition 2017

1 2 3 4 5 6 7 8 9 10

052717

For
Christy and Steve Ruiz
Heidi and Matt Hilton
Jon and Torie McBirney
Cody and Taylor Fields

If no one else ever read this book, we still would have written it for you. You were on our minds and in our hearts with every word. You are our inspiration. We are so very proud to be your dads and fathers-in-law. Know that we are cheering you on during every step of your marriages.

CONTENTS

Part One: Your Journey Together

Part Two: Eight Gauges for a Great Marriage

FOREWORD

Some things you can learn before the wedding. However, most of the skills required for a long-term, healthy marriage are learned in the first few years of marriage. Many couples enter marriage thinking, *We love each other and we are going to make each other happy.* However, when they come down off the emotional high of the "in love" experience, they find they are not always inclined to "make each other happy."

All of us come to marriage with expectations and visions of what it will be like. Most of us find marriage is not what we thought it would be. In an effort to be more realistic, some couples decide to live together before they get married. The idea is to do a "trial run" and see how it goes. While this may seem logical, research indicates that most of these couples end up not getting married. Those who do marry have a higher divorce rate than those who do not live together before the wedding.

The truth is, marriage cannot be simulated. It is a covenant relationship in which we proclaim privately and publicly that we will stand by each other in sickness and in health, in poverty and in wealth, and we will keep our relationship exclusive, so long as we shall live. It is a sobering commitment which brings great security for the couple who takes their vows seriously. However, working out the daily details can be tricky.

I have never met a couple who got married intending to make each other miserable. Yet my office and those of other counselors are filled with couples who are very unhappy. The reality is, we must learn how to create a loving, caring, supportive relationship. It does not happen simply by doing "what comes naturally."

That is why the book you hold in your hands is so important. It will give you the benefit of learning from two counselors who are honest about their own journeys to successful marriages and have counseled with thousands of other couples through the years. Their advice is practical and doable. Wherever you are in your marital journey, you will find their ideas helpful in building a mutually satisfying marriage.

What you do in the first few years of your marriage, if you make wise decisions, will open the doorway to a successful marriage. Once you learn how to work as a team, each supporting the other, you will find the marriage you've always wanted.

Gary Chapman, Ph.D., author
of *The 5 Love Languages*

ACKNOWLEDGMENTS

Thank you …

- Cindy Ward: Your incredible help and positive attitude make it a joy to work with you. Thank you so much for all your extra touches with this project.
- Heather McGrath and Alisha Ballard: You have been so very supportive of so many of the latest HomeWord initiatives. We are deeply honored by your involvement.
- Rod Emery, Tom Purcell, and Randy Bramel: Your long-term leadership always goes far beyond what is expected. A thousand thanks.
- Steve and Sue Perry: You started something with the Refreshing Your Marriage movement and its continual success points back to you.
- Fadi Cheikha: We are so grateful for your friendship, your encouragement, and for being so gracious to provide office space.

- Jeff Maguire: Thank you for being our pastor and fueling us with amazing teaching from God's Word.
- Ted Lowe and Ted Cunningham: You have been so kind to share your marriage advice with open hands. We look forward to many more years of working together.
- Cathy Burns and Cathy Fields: The help that couples will receive from this book would have never been possible without your inspiration and love.

INTRODUCTION

Your early years of marriage are foundational years. The decisions, habits, and values you establish during that time will often determine the success and happiness of your relationship for the long haul. These crucial years are so very important.

The problem with many marriages today is that they are so busy and distracted by other "important commitments" that they drift from the very actions that made them want to get married. This drift is quite common but can become dangerous to your marriage if some course corrections are not implemented along the marriage journey. This is a book about identifying the drift and developing the skills needed to make the corrections that will lead to a healthy marriage—the one we know you want.

As we wrote this book for you, two thoughts were at the forefront of our minds: 1) We wished we would have had a book like this when we were first married. Every time we tell someone we are writing a book about the first few years of marriage, we get the same response. "Where was this book when we were first married?" 2) Even if no one else reads this book, we would still have written it—just for our own children. Four of our combined six kids are in the first few years of their marriages, so this quickly became a very personal project for us.

We loved writing this and thinking of all the couples it will help. We strongly believe it can strengthen any couple's marriage, even if they aren't in their first few years. Much of the content comes out of our own life experiences, research, and being fortunate enough to be married to two of the finest women in the universe. We are honored you are reading this, and we would love to hear what has been helpful to you. Write to us at Info@HomeWord.com.

HOW TO GET THE MOST OUT OF *THE FIRST FEW YEARS OF MARRIAGE*:

Read the book with your spouse. Whether you both read it separately and then come together to talk about it or read it together and discuss it, try to engage as a couple. We hope you can create shared goals and a common language that can help your marriage thrive.

Consider going through this with a small group. We have created a workbook and video (find the curriculum at **HomeWord.com/FirstFewYears**) that can be used in a small group with other couples. You can learn so much more from others who are exploring the same topics and doing life together.

Work through the book and video curriculum with a "marriage mentor" couple. We are big believers in the effectiveness of mentors. We encourage you to find an older, wiser, more experienced couple and ask them to go through the content with you. Their insight could be life changing. With *The First Few Years of Marriage* video curriculum, there is a special message for marriage mentors.

No matter how you use this book, it's our hope and prayer that it helps you make your marriage a priority and guides you to develop the skills needed to thrive in your relationship. We hope you'll enjoy this book as much as we enjoyed writing it.

Blessings,
Jim and Doug

Part One

•

YOUR JOURNEY TOGETHER

Chapter One

•

ONE MARRIAGE, MANY DRIFTS, THOUSANDS OF COURSE CORRECTIONS

We wish we could sit with you and hear your favorite memories and stories from your wedding day.

Your wedding day may rank as one of the most incredible days of your life, and if a beautiful wedding day were an indicator of a healthy married life, this book wouldn't be needed. But it is, because a great wedding doesn't equate to a great marriage.

This book is less about your wedding and more about your relationship now that you're married. We're big fans of great weddings, but we're even bigger fans of great marriages. That's why we're excited about helping you thrive in your marriage.

By now your honeymoon has passed, and the long-term journey of your marriage is moving forward. Chances are you've already experienced some ups and downs in your early days, months, or years together, and the very fact that you're reading this book reveals that you care about the health of your marriage. That's a good starting point.

Think of your marriage as a journey and ask yourselves this question: "Are we prepared for a fifty-year voyage?" It's okay if you're not sure. We definitely weren't when we married!

Cathy and I (Jim) were so focused on planning our dream wedding that we didn't give much thought to our upcoming life together. Like so many couples, we spent a great deal of time, money, and energy on our ceremony without giving significant consideration to the many years that would follow—especially fifty years. We should have thought more deeply about what was to come. It's not as if we didn't have a plethora of premarital resources available to help us navigate future reality. Today, there are even more outstanding premarital resources and advice, including the book Doug and I wrote titled *Getting Ready for Marriage* (but of course we're a little biased). The problem wasn't that wisdom and advice weren't available before Cathy and I got married; we just weren't ready for it. Can you relate to that, at least a little?

Cathy and I married in 1974, and the first few years of marriage were challenging! To be honest, there were moments I wanted to run away by myself to another country and never return. There were times of disappointment, frustration, and unmet expectations, but there were amazing, hopeful, and beautiful times as well. Our first few years weren't all bad, but they weren't all good either.

I (Doug) married my wife, Cathy, in 1985, and the first few years of our marriage were amazing! (Yes, Jim and I married two incredible women who share the same name.) Of course we had to make adjustments, but we often look back at those years with a great deal of joy and gratitude for the way we began our marriage. The foundation we laid during those early years was essential to the long-term success of our marital relationship.

Jim and I talk to so many newly married couples who admit that they should have asked more significant questions and given deeper thought to life after saying "I do." Truthfully, even if you did ask great questions before marriage, you probably have even more questions now—and different ones. That's good!

In the pages that follow, we hope to answer many of your questions, as well as ones you haven't even thought of yet. We felt compelled to write this book to help you win in your marriage. You may have had a great wedding, but now let's explore how you can have a great marriage.

IS DESIRE ENOUGH?

Both of us have performed hundreds of weddings and talked with thousands of couples about their marriages, and we're strongly convinced that how you build your marriage foundation during these first few years is the primary factor for long-term happiness and marital success. Research backs up that statement: couples who persevere through the first few years of marriage are much more likely to have long, happy, and lasting relationships with their spouses.[1]

We're going to assume you agree that learning about marriage, developing new relational skills, and putting those skills into practice are critical to the future health of your marriage and are important parts of growing as a spouse. We feel safe making that assumption because you're reading this book. We want to congratulate you for your desire to learn about being successful in marriage. Desire is an essential foundational action that makes all the difference in a marriage. Without the desire to grow, learn, and change, you'll drift from your intended destination and what's most important in your marriage.

Brian and Jenny had desire, but it was focused in the wrong direction. They became a busy, distracted young married couple. They met right out of college, dated for two and a half years, got engaged, and quickly married. Two years later, they were surprised to discover that Jenny was pregnant. They hadn't planned on having a baby so soon, and they weren't prepared for the changes that would entail. Their marriage was experiencing a subtle yet unresolved tension, and they knew a baby was only going to inflame the issues that were bubbling under the surface.

Thankfully they realized it wasn't too late to shift their misplaced desire from their vocations and focus instead on improving their relationship. They read a couple of marriage books, got into counseling, participated in a couples' conference, and joined a small group from their church. Fortunately, Jenny's pregnancy triggered a desire in both of them to emphasize their marriage. The effort Brian and Jenny put into improving their marriage as a result of Jenny's pregnancy has paid off, and they now enjoy a happier, healthier, and deeper relationship.

Jenny's pregnancy served as a wake-up call for their marriage. They admitted to us that they had simply stopped doing some of the things they knew would benefit their marriage. They hadn't intentionally stopped; it was an innocent "We just got too busy and distracted" stop. This phenomenon is so very common in the marriages we study that we refer to it as *the drift*. When Brian and Jenny stopped desiring to grow, learn, and change as a couple, they began to drift from their intended destination. An undercurrent of apathy moved them away from the promises they made to each other on their wedding day.

Here's what's tricky: The drift sneaks up on couples. It gradually pulls husbands and wives apart and moves them away from their intended target of a healthy marriage. At first the drift doesn't seem as if it's even happening. It's deceptive. Couples go about their ordinary daily lives, becoming busy and preoccupied, and when they have a wake-up call (like Brian and Jenny) or a relational blowup, they look at each other and realize their marriage has drifted off course.

THE SLOW DRIFT

We both live in Southern California and have had the privilege of growing up near the beach. More times than we can recall, we've headed to the ocean to cool off or play or ride a wave, and before we know it, the undercurrent has shifted us farther down the shore. If you've never experienced this before, it might be hard to imagine, but it's true for anyone who spends time in the sea. The drift has no racial, religious, or socioeconomic bias. If you're in the ocean, you'll inevitably drift from where you started.

Imagine that your marriage is a boat. You can choose the style—sailboat, motorboat, rowboat, speedboat, or tugboat. It doesn't matter. Your marriage boat is pointed toward an intended destination. Let's pretend you're planning to sail to the island of your dreams. This is the location you intended to reach when you first thought of being married to one person for the rest of your life. To get there, you charted out a course and planned to arrive at your final destination in fifty years. (That's a great marriage-anniversary number.) Now imagine that as you set out on your journey, you're just one degree off course. One degree doesn't seem like very much, but over a long period of time, you'll totally miss your destination and could shipwreck your marriage.

On your marriage journey, you'll need to be aware of the undercurrent and keep an eye on your navigation devices, or you'll miss your destination. To be very honest, we're both sick and tired of watching marriages drift off course and shipwreck. Too many couples experience this very real marriage drift and then look up one day to discover they're lost and stranded on the island of hopelessness. They began a beautiful journey on their wedding day but slowly drifted off course because their misguided desires took their focus off their destination, and they weren't wise or courageous enough to make the necessary adjustments to get back on course. We don't want that to happen to you!

MARRIAGE IS ABOUT COURSE CORRECTIONS

In nautical or aviation terms, adjustments are called *course corrections*. Throughout this book we'll be referring to the drift and course corrections in our marriages.

I (Jim) spoke recently in Houston, Texas, where I had the privilege of meeting an astronaut. It was quite the thrill! He shared with me a fascinating fact about space travel: "Our people at NASA are in control of our flights about 3 percent of the time, and 97 percent of the time, we [astronauts] are just [making] course corrections."

There's such a strong parallel to marriage in that statement. Think about your dating and engagement months as 3 percent of your relationship. Ninety-seven percent is your marriage relationship. That's the percentage of time you'll spend making course corrections to ensure you'll reach your target. Your marriage journey has the potential to be out of this world (think of the incredible views from space), but it also has the potential to crash if you don't make thousands of small (and occasionally large) course corrections along the way.

The course corrections we'll suggest in this book are all doable. The skills and habits you develop early in your marriage will minimize the need to make the same course corrections later. As a matter of fact, we believe you'll become so proficient at making course corrections that a healthy, vibrant, abundant, alive, and awesome marriage will always be within reach.

SOME ACTION REQUIRED

A wife accompanied her husband of twenty-five years to the doctor's office because he had been feeling ill for a couple of weeks and was under tremendous stress. She stayed in the waiting room for what seemed like an extremely long time while the doctor poked, prodded, questioned, and took blood and urine samples from her husband. Finally, the doctor came to the waiting room and motioned for the woman to follow him into his office for a one-on-one conversation.

As soon as the woman sat down, the doctor blurted out, "Your husband is severely ill. I'm afraid he might not make it if you don't take some extreme measures over the next year."

The wife was shocked. She knew her husband was sick but had no idea it was that severe.

She asked the doctor, "What can I do to keep him from dying?"

The doctor answered, "Stress is killing him, so to save his life, you'll have to cook him a warm breakfast every day before he leaves for work. When he returns home, he'll need pleasant, stress-free time with your children. They shouldn't yell, argue, or fight when they're with him. You'll also need to take over all the family discipline, and it's essential that you refrain from nagging or expressing any type of negativity."

The wife sat there speechless as the doctor continued. "I also suggest you meet all of your husband's sexual needs on a regular basis. If you can do all of this over the next year, I'm confident your husband will fully regain his health."

The woman was stunned when she left the office.

On the car ride home, the husband asked his wife, "What did the doctor say to you about my illness?"

She paused, gazed out the window, and calmly said, "You're gonna die."

Here's the principle connected to that silly joke: we can write a book prescribing course corrections both of you can take to keep your marriage alive and healthy, but it's going to require more than simply reading these ideas. To keep your marriage from drifting, you'll need to take action—even some courageous actions. Your marriage can easily drift to a dangerous place if you're not *intentionally* thinking and talking about the issues we write about in the following chapters.

There's great hope for couples who are willing to invest time and energy in making their marriages thrive, especially in the first few years. We want to help you do this, and with more than seventy-five years of combined marriage experience, we have some suggestions that can help you navigate some of the choppy waters you'll encounter along the way.

We're thrilled you're up for this voyage. Let's set sail. Bon voyage!

QUESTIONS

1. How would you rate your general marriage satisfaction on a scale of 1 (miserable) to 10 (amazing)?

2. What are you currently doing right in your marriage that you hope to continue doing fifty years from now?

3. What course corrections do you think you might need to implement to improve your relationship and keep your marriage from drifting? (Don't worry, we'll offer some ideas in the next several chapters.)

Chapter Two

•

HAPPINESS IS A CHOICE

On the day I (Jim) stood before my family and friends and exchanged vows with Cathy, I had no idea of the magnitude of what I was getting myself into. I did know I was in love and that Cathy was beyond beautiful both inside and out. Yet I had no way of knowing that this decision would be filled with such powerful emotions and long-term ramifications.

I'd been excited about marriage, but it was simply too future oriented for me to fully embrace. There was no context for me to forecast what our life together would be like. I hadn't spent much time thinking about eating thousands of meals together, making love countless times, raising children from birth to adulthood, going on vacations as a family, arguing with each other, making huge financial decisions together, and essentially aligning all our important dreams and goals. I loved Cathy deeply, but honestly, I didn't grasp how big and complex marriage would be.

For good or bad, our worlds would intermingle, and much of my day, whether I was with her or not, would be centered around Cathy and her needs. Even forty years later, it still seems mind-blowing that I committed to be with this person "till death do us part." It also seems crazy to admit that I'm still learning to love her well, and every day of marriage presents new opportunities for me to be a more gracious and loving husband. One of the biggest lessons I've learned along the way is that a successful marriage is all about choices.

BASIC PRINCIPLES FOR A HEALTHY MARRIAGE

Seventy-five years' worth of combined marriage experience and continuing education with our wives have given birth to some marriage principles that Doug and I are excited to share with you. As we gathered ideas for this book, we quickly established the drift metaphor as the primary image and language we want you to keep in mind as you reflect on your own marriage. We then identified eight gauges to help you stay on course and minimize the drift in your marriage. Try to imagine different types of gauges that are valuable on any sea voyage: depth gauge, temperature gauge, tension gauge, fuel gauge, trim gauge, air-pressure gauge, and so on. You get the idea. Likewise, gauges can help keep you from drifting too far off course in your marriage.

Before we introduce these gauges in part 2, we want to convey three foundational marriage principles that are important for you to understand before your voyage takes you too far out to sea. Think of these principles as the basic sailing instructions you'll need to rely on and return to throughout your marriage voyage. The gauges will keep you heading in the right direction, but they won't do a lot of good if you don't know some of the basic principles of sailing. Essentially, these principles are the three basics you need to know for a happy, healthy marriage.

Vince Lombardi of the Green Bay Packers was one of the greatest football coaches of all time. Among his most memorable statements was "When you get away from the fundamentals, you've gone a long way toward defeat." Wise words that were meant for a bunch of football players are also true when it comes to marriage. Most marriages don't derail because of infidelity; instead, they slowly drift and dissolve when days and months of straying from the basic principles of a strong and healthy marriage turn into seasons and years.

Let's consider the basics before we dive into a discussion of the different gauges.

1. A HAPPY, HEALTHY MARRIAGE IS A CHOICE, NOT A COINCIDENCE.

The sooner you embrace this truth, the better your marriage will be. A marriage filled with happiness doesn't just happen naturally. Happiness is a choice, and you always have the power to choose a different outcome. You make hundreds of choices every day about things like sock color, hair products, food, and television channels. Obviously, there are many other more important choices you'll make that have the potential to change you and your marriage.

Love is a choice. You can choose to love your spouse in big and small ways every day, even when you don't feel like it, since love isn't just a feeling. You have the freedom to choose how you'll respond when your feelings are hurt, when expectations are unmet, or when you feel you've been misunderstood. This may seem like an over-simplification, but a good marriage isn't just two people with good chemistry. It's two people who affect each other by making good choices. It's that simple—and that complex.

Marriage experts report that even in the most troubled marriages, if couples *choose* to persevere and work on their issues, at least 75 percent will be better off in five years.[1] Unfortunately, many couples in troubled marriages either give up too soon or are unwilling to make the necessary choices to improve their marriages. Journalist Kin Hubbard once said, "It's pretty hard to find what does bring happiness. Poverty and wealth have both failed." True happiness in marriage isn't about money; it's about choices. If money were the secret to a great marriage, there would never be divorces in Hollywood.

In their book *Making Happy: The Art and Science of a Happy Marriage*, Les and Leslie Parrott talk about the "happiness pie," which University of California professor David Schkade and colleagues developed from a review of multiple studies to illustrate the factors that determine happiness.[2]

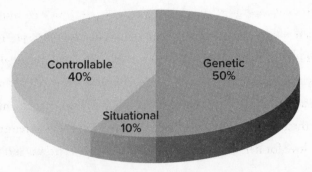

The premise of the happiness pie is that 50 percent of your life is made up of genetic factors over which you have no control. This "biological set point" includes family history, personality, and other hereditary factors. Situational factors like health, family-related issues, jobs, and other negative or positive circumstances make up 10 percent of your life. Think of this as the "stuff" that happens to you, over which you have little or no control. The final 40 percent of your life can be attributed to the choices you make, which are entirely under your control.

That's an encouraging statistic because it means you have much more control over your marriage than you think you do! Happiness in marriage doesn't depend on your spouse. It depends on your choices.

Do you want to increase your happiness quotient? Of course you do! Here's the easiest way to get started: choose to be thankful. Make gratitude a habit. That's a sign of a healthy marriage! Dr. Greg and Erin Smalley tell us that if we practice gratitude in our marriages, our happiness level rises as much as 25 percent.[3] That's a huge spike in happiness, and it's directly connected to thankfulness!

One anniversary, I (Jim) wrote down one hundred reasons I was grateful for Cathy and then cut the pages into one hundred little scraps of paper and gave them to her in a decorative jar. It was one of the most powerful gifts I've ever given her. Although the little strips of paper have long since yellowed, they're still sitting on her bedroom dresser. She saved those words of encouragement and views them as a treasure. She'll occasionally read them as reminders of my love for her, but the irony is that while this gift was intended for Cathy, it also reminded me of the many reasons I love her. It was a double win that illustrates the power of choosing gratitude and putting it into action.

Have you ever heard the story of the man who was invited to his boss's home for lunch? After a lovely meal, the boss complimented his wife, thanking her for all her hard work on the meal, and then he volunteered himself and his employee to clean up the kitchen.

While they were doing the dishes, the employee asked, "Why do you treat your wife so well?"

His boss simply replied, "Because she deserves it, and it makes our marriage happier."

The employee was so impressed with what his boss had done that he decided to express thankfulness to his wife later that night.

When he got home, he said, "Honey, you look wonderful. I'm the luckiest guy in the world to have you as my wife. I love you so much."

Immediately his wife burst into tears.

When he asked, "What's wrong?" she replied, "Our son got in a fight at school today, I got a speeding ticket, the refrigerator is busted, and now you've come home drunk!"

This old joke underscores the value of showing gratitude on a more regular basis. When you express gratitude, you don't want your spouse thinking you're intoxicated or trying to butter her up. Make the choice to express gratitude, and you'll find yourself and your marriage in a happier place. That's what good choices do—they provide the course corrections you need in your marriage.

Prepare yourself. You'll be reading a lot about choices in this book.

2. YOU CAN'T CHANGE YOUR SPOUSE; YOU CAN ONLY CHANGE YOURSELF.

Have you ever played the If Only game? Here's how it goes:

- *"If only* my spouse were more outgoing …"
- *"If only* she would stop spending money …"
- *"If only* my husband was more romantic …"

You get the idea. "If only" projects your wish list upon your spouse. Most married couples have played this dreadful game, including us, but it never nets any relational wins. It's just a bad fantasy role-play that doesn't inspire a healthy marriage.

What does lead to a healthy marriage is realizing you can't change each other. You can only change yourself. The If Only game is useless. If you want a great marriage, you must focus on the choices you can make to change yourself. Usually the first step in changing yourself is changing your attitude. Your circumstances may never change, but your attitude can change, and transforming your attitude can transform your marriage.

Dustin and Destiny had been married for four years and had a one-year-old baby boy. One evening Dustin came home late from work—*again*. Destiny was fuming. Their conflict escalated into another major fight. Nothing was resolved, and Dustin slept on the couch. The next day Destiny packed some things and took the baby to her mother's house.

She complained to her mom, "I'm thinking about leaving Dustin. He is so inconsiderate. Since we've had the baby, he seems to work all the time, and our communication is terrible. I'm always so mad at him."

Her mother's advice was profound. "Honey, I understand what it's like to be mad at your husband. I really do! However, before you make such a drastic decision, I'd like to challenge you to write down every good trait that Dustin possesses. I know firsthand that he has some really great qualities, and I can remember you bragging about them when you were dating. After you finish that list, I want you to make a second column and write all the ways you might be playing a part in the pain of your relationship. This exercise has helped give me perspective. Whenever I struggle with your father, I recall the advice I learned from Jesus back in my Sunday-school days, and instead of pointing out all your father's faults, I look at mine first."

Destiny's mom was referring to these profound words:

> Why do you look at the speck of sawdust in your [spouse's] eye and pay no attention to the plank in your own eye? How can you say to your [spouse], "Let me take the speck out of your eye," when all the time there is a plank in your own eye? You hypocrite, first take the plank out of your own eye, and then you will see clearly to remove the speck from your [spouse's] eye.[4]

Destiny didn't want to hear her mom's or Jesus's words, but she reluctantly completed the assignment. She listed Dustin's good traits in one column and then wrote a longer list of the ways she was sabotaging their relationship. This exercise exposed a painful truth: Destiny was as much a part of the problem as Dustin.

After taking some personal time to reflect on their marriage, she asked if her mom would take care of the baby so she could have some alone time with Dustin. Destiny returned home, cleaned the house, put on a nice dress, fixed herself up, and cooked Dustin's favorite meal. When he came home from work, she greeted him with an apology and a kiss. During dinner, she read both lists to him and explained what she learned about herself through this exercise. She chose the route of humility and courageously owned her part in their relational pain.

Dustin listened carefully and then apologized for his role in their conflict. They both agreed that making up is a lot more fun than sleeping on the couch.

The If Only game has just one player, but Destiny recognized that there are always two players in the conflict game. She realized that she is 100 percent responsible for how she responds and 0 percent responsible for how Dustin responds. She needed to be reminded that she can't control Dustin's actions, but she can choose her response. That's a very important marriage principle to understand.

Early in my (Doug's) marriage, I tried to change some things that bugged me about Cathy. It never worked, however, and always led to pain, frustration, and additional conflict. Friends who had been married longer offered wise counsel and told me it was useless, but I tried to change her anyway. It seemed as though the harder I tried, the more agony I brought into our marriage. Although I never used the word *defective*, I was clearly communicating to Cathy that she wasn't right the way she was. I was so immature.

Now, instead of trying to change her, I know the most productive route is choosing to change my attitude. It really works! I can't control her, but I can choose to grow up and not allow petty things to bug me. Cathy and I can talk about whatever frustrates me, and I can explain why it does, but I can't ultimately change her. The same is true in your marriage. The only person you can change is yourself. Start there every time!

3. A SUCCESSFUL MARRIAGE REQUIRES SERVING EACH OTHER AND FALLING IN LOVE AGAIN EVERY DAY.

I (Doug) remember the exact moment I looked into the eyes of my own Cathy and knew it was love. It was a powerful and transforming moment. It was the same for Jim.

If you want a healthy marriage, you must discipline yourself to fall in love with your spouse over and over again. This action is a continual choice. There's that word again. The choice to keep falling in love is less about romantic feelings and more about *routine actions*. According to the *Oxford English Dictionary Online*, *routine* refers to an action that is "performed as part of a regular procedure rather than for a special reason." This definition fits marriage perfectly. You don't choose to love your spouse for a special reason. Instead, you love your spouse for no reason at all. That's what love is. It doesn't demand a reason.

True love is sacrificial, and if you want to become a better lover, you'll learn to *serve* your spouse daily. Serving others is the ultimate sacrifice. It means laying down our lives for someone else.[5] The apostle Paul's letter to the people of Ephesus offers solid marriage advice: "Submit to one another out of reverence for Christ."[6] The word *submit* also means "to serve." When you have a servant's attitude toward your spouse, you are literally acting like Jesus. Serving is your choice: you can choose to be either a servant lover or a selfish lover. If you're a servant lover, you'll look for ways to serve your spouse through simple, routine, ordinary acts of kindness. You'll do it for no special reason or payback; instead, you'll serve as an expression of your love for your spouse. You can fall in love every day and express that love in practical acts of service.

Following her husband's death after forty-six years of marriage, Sue Johnston wrote, "Four children, 46 bouquets [of flowers] and a lifetime of love were his legacy to me when he passed away." She continued, "On my first Valentine's Day … ten months after I lost him, I was shocked to receive a gorgeous bouquet from [my husband]. Angry and heartbroken, I called the florist to say there had been a mistake."

The florist responded, "No, ma'am, it's not a mistake. Before he passed away, your husband prepaid for many years and asked us to guarantee that you'd continue getting bouquets every Valentine's Day." The attached card read, "My love for you is eternal."[7]

That thoughtful, incredible husband chose to serve his wife "till death do us part" and beyond. He was a servant lover. You can experience a healthy marriage like that no matter what circumstances you're currently facing.

All three of these basic marriage instructions begin with a choice: choose happiness, choose to focus on changing yourself instead of your spouse, and choose to fall in love over and over, expressing that love through servanthood. When you make these choices consistently and don't stray from them, you'll experience a healthier, more successful marriage.

As you learn about the marriage gauges in the following chapters, we hope you'll revisit these very important principles and allow them to guide your marriage well into the future.

QUESTIONS

1. What proactive choices could you make to improve your marriage relationship?
2. Do you ever play the If Only game? If so, what are your most common "if only" thoughts about your spouse (e.g., *If only he or she would* …)? What can you do to change your attitude?
3. List the top four qualities your spouse possesses that you're thankful for.

Part Two

•

EIGHT GAUGES FOR
A GREAT MARRIAGE

Chapter Three

•

LAUGH DAILY AND DATE WEEKLY

No doubt you've heard the expression "Laughter is good medicine." That same idea is also found in Scripture: "A cheerful heart is good medicine, but a broken spirit saps a person's strength."[1] We believe with all our heart that this is a truism for marriage as well. This may sound like an oversimplification, but couples who have fun and laugh together often enjoy a deep and gratifying relational connection. Our hope is that your marriage will be filled with a deep sense of confidence that comes from fun and laughter and spending enjoyable moments together.

THE IMPORTANCE OF FUN AND LAUGHTER

One of the reasons fun and laughter are so important for your future as a couple is because marriage isn't the easiest of relationships.

You've likely experienced that already. When the lives of two messy, broken, sinful people collide, there's bound to be some chaos and pain. No one ever promised that marriage would be easy. Your relationship will experience pressure and stress, your life will most likely be filled with busyness and complications, and your marriage will pay a price for that type of pressure-cooker reality. As a result, you'll need to relieve some of the stress you feel with each other, and nothing works faster and better than including laughter and fun in your relational script.

How would you describe the current fun factor in your marriage? If you've been drifting a little in this area, you're in good company. Even if your fun factor is good, please don't stop reading, because an exciting challenge is waiting for you later in this chapter.

One evening my (Jim's) daughter Heidi came home from baby-sitting for a couple Cathy and I have known since they were in our youth group many years ago. Cathy and I were sitting at the kitchen table paying bills when Heidi bounced in, sat down, and announced, "I love Scott and Anita and their kids. I had no idea you guys were their youth leaders when they were in high school." At that point she paused with a look of confusion on her face. "They also said you guys *used to be* fun and funny." Her facial expression basically said, "How long ago was that, and what happened?"

Oh, my, that statement hurt! After she left the room, I looked at Cathy and said, "You know, we really were more fun back in those days. We've drifted from fun and have become too serious. We need to reinvent ourselves and get back to having more fun."

Cathy agreed but didn't want to start until *after* we finished paying the bills.

That night became a turning point for us because we made a conscious choice to start having more fun with our family and, particularly, in our marriage. I knew we needed to make some course corrections immediately, or we'd be stuck in the same old rut, and fun would be just another good idea disappearing in our rearview mirror.

The next night, Cathy and I wrote down several fun things we could do as a family over the next six months, and we made another list of what Cathy and I could do as a couple. We then instituted Monday funday and intentionally started including more fun activities in our lives.

What Cathy and I learned, I pass on to you before your fun drift happens. Sometimes a couple simply has to stop, drive a stake of commitment into the ground, and become proactive about developing the fun factor in their marriage. You may need to do that right now (or after you pay the bills and finish reading this chapter).

Research has found that strong emotional connections are formed more often from having fun together than from checking items off a to-do list or telling each other what's wrong with your relationship. We're not sure how much those researchers got paid to uncover that information, but you don't need a PhD to understand the truth behind their discovery. Fun is fun! When fun is evident in a marriage, couples communicate more effectively. You want your spouse to talk more? Then have more fun!

Typically, couples want to talk their way out of their problems because they believe *words* are the answer. We're not suggesting that couples shouldn't talk; rather, we believe couples need to have fun together, and when that happens, the needed words will come.

Words don't always lead to a stronger connection, but a stronger connection will lead to more words. Trying to force connection through communication is tough.

Cathy and I (Doug) find that when we're hanging out on a trail and walking or jogging, we have deeper and more honest conversations than when we're sitting in the kitchen because "we have to talk about this issue now." Communication and connection flow better when we're more relaxed, hanging out together, and having fun. Having fun together isn't just a good idea or an added perk for your marriage when you have the time. It's essential to a healthy marriage. One of the best ways to protect your marriage is to enjoy each other. Please don't underestimate the power of fun.

Several years ago, I (Jim) wrote a book called *10 Building Blocks for a Solid Family*. While researching happy and successful families, I discovered that playing together was one of the essential factors for developing a healthy, close-knit family.[2] Those who intentionally took time to incorporate play into their family time thrived, while families who didn't value playing together tended to be less satisfied in their primary relationships. The glue that made healthy families stick together seemed to be the additional element of play.

This principle is also true for you as you strive to build a successful marriage. Playing together, expressing humor, laughing, and having fun will not only establish a foundation of memories you'll return to when times are tough, but they will also unite your hearts and help you heal the wounds that are part of every marriage. Fun and playfulness will become deposits of love that you can bank on when the negative withdrawals happen. Laughter and fun can bring healing to a hurting marriage.

Are you convinced yet? Are you ready to add more fun and laughter into your marriage journey? Are you excited to drive that stake into the ground and commit to being a couple that is intentional about having fun? We sure hope so! If you're ready to start having fun in your marriage, here is the number-one way to do it consistently: date often.

WEEKLY DATES

At our marriage conferences, Doug and I typically ask how many couples have a weekly date, and it saddens us to see only a few raised hands. Then we ask, "How many of you had weekly dates when you were dating and engaged?" Boom! Almost everyone raises their hands and sheepishly glances at their spouses with a look that says, "Remember that? That was fun!"

What happened? Why is it that couples who say "I do" on their wedding day find themselves saying "We don't" when it comes to dating? Marriage isn't a club to join so you can stop paying for dates. Dating got you *to* marriage, and we would argue that dating your mate helps you *do* marriage in a more beautiful and enjoyable way.

Here's the bottom line: couples who date their spouses regularly have more intimate and satisfying marriages. Please understand, a date with your spouse isn't the same as going out to dinner to talk about all your issues. We're not suggesting you go on a date so you can work on your marriage and ask deep questions like "What are the three biggest needs in our relationship, and how can I better meet them?" While those might be important questions to ask each other, we would label that as *work*. Dates don't always need an agenda. You don't always have to work on your marriage to have a great one.

Author Leonard Sweet said, "For a marriage to sing and dance, for two people to make beautiful music together, they need to play, not work, at their marriage."[3]

If you're like most of the people at our marriage conferences, you might be thinking, *Come on, guys, I get the fun piece, but dating every week? Are you serious? What planet do you live on?*

We hear that every time we present this challenge. Yes, we're serious. Very serious. Weekly dating sounds like a lot, but as residents of Planet Healthy Marriage, we want you to be our neighbors. Yes, we realize that *weekly* comes around every seven days, but the power of this challenge is the consistency needed to turn dating into a habit. Dating each other is one of the areas of marriage that will require you to look each other in the eyes and say, "We need to do this."

You'll need to develop some new time patterns if dating hasn't been part of your weekly routine. You'll also have to face your excuses honestly and come up with rational responses that shatter each one. We'll help you get started, because we've heard all the excuses couples give for not dating. Here are the top three:

1. "We're too busy." We know busy! We're both busy people who live full and active lives with kids, grandkids, speaking engagements, book deadlines, companies to run, consulting, and more. We get it. We acknowledge you're also busy, but we'd ask you to remove the word *too* from your excuse. When you do, it changes from an excuse to a statement of fact: "We're really busy, but our busyness isn't more important than our relationship."

If Doug and I were sitting across the table from you and your spouse at a restaurant, and we asked, "Could you agree to giving each other 1 percent of your time on a weekly basis?" we hope you would say yes. (If you didn't, we might "accidentally" spill our water on you.) Come on! It's only 1 percent. One percent of your weekly time equals only one hour and forty minutes. In math lingo, that's 1,440 minutes a day x 7 days = 10,080 minutes a week x 1% = 1 hour, 40 minutes.

Yes, you're busy. Maybe even very busy. But if you want a healthy marriage, it will require learning to discern what you do with your time, how you invest it, and what time investments will give you the best returns. Dating weekly is a very wise investment of your time. (By the way, it doesn't have to be a date *night*; it could be a date *morning* or *afternoon*.)

2. "We don't have the money." There is no rule that says your date must be fancy or expensive. You may have gone that route when you were dating or engaged, but don't allow finances to become an excuse now. The biggest expense will usually be your time. You can go on a walk together, watch a Little League game of five-year-old kids trying to play baseball, or take a cup of coffee into a fancy hotel lobby and sit there for free. Go on Pinterest. com, type "cheap dates" in the search window, and you'll discover hundreds of ideas. Money isn't what makes a date special. If having money guaranteed a strong marriage, we'd never see professional athletes divorce. It's not the money; it's the time. Get rid of this excuse and begin thinking of free and cheap dates. Someday you may be able to afford fancier dates, but the low- or no-cost ones will trigger just as many fond memories.

3. "We can't find a babysitter." Before we address the babysitter excuse, we want to comment on *child-centric marriages*. Once children enter the equation, marriage definitely becomes more difficult. (We'll discuss this more thoroughly in chapter 9.) A child-centric marriage occurs when one or both spouses view the kids as more important than the marriage. Even when couples won't admit it, their actions often reveal the truth. A child-focused marriage can take your time and attention away from each other.

Some of our young married friends will say, "But Doug and Jim, my kids are always so needy. I can address my spouse's needs later." While that may be true, it's a recipe for disaster, because "later" often gets lost. In fact, that word is what ignites the drift. "Later" creeps in and slowly, subtly influences decisions and actions. Couples who say "We'll do it later" blink and discover that years have passed, and they find themselves acting more like roommates than romantic partners. That outcome begins with an innocent and sincere desire to be good parents. The motive is right, but the execution is wrong. A kid-centric marriage leads to trouble.

We know of a couple who had six children, and they figured out how to have a special date with each child every week, but they hadn't been on a date as a couple for more than five years. When they told us about their marriage, the tears in their eyes revealed that they were good parents, but they had drifted apart and become disconnected as husband and wife and now felt distant from each other. Their children came before their marriage. It shouldn't be that way!

If you have children, we're thrilled, but we want them to be excited that their parents have a healthy marriage and put their relationship before their parenting. Yes, having children can be an excuse.

But it's just not strong enough to sway us from issuing the challenge to date weekly. You've probably heard it said before: "Excuses are like armpits. We all have them, and they usually stink."

If you can't afford babysitting, then offer to trade with another couple: you take their kids one time, and they take yours another time. Or schedule at-home dates once the kids are asleep. You can do that for an hour and forty minutes every week. We know it's not easy, but having a strong, healthy, vibrant marriage isn't going to just happen.

By the way, dating isn't just a good idea we're challenging you to embrace because it's worked for our marriages. The research on dating supports our claims. For example, the University of Virginia's National Marriage Project identified five key ways that dating leads to increased marital satisfaction.[4]

1. Dating keeps the lines of communication open in marriage. With mobile devices left in the car and attentive behavior on display, a date allows extended time for emotional connection. We've already mentioned that it's important to guard against expecting deep, intense conversations about marital issues. You might want to save conversations that have the potential to get heated for another time. Since you're going to commit to a weekly date night, it might also be wise to set aside another time each week to discuss finances, the family calendar, and kid issues. That way, you don't have to deliberate on them on your date night.

2. Dating is the perfect time for couples to try something new. This is where you go against the grain and break the routine of dinner and a movie. If you're not doing anything, start with dinner and a movie. But don't go there every week. Occasionally doing something new will help you develop a stronger bond as you share in experiences that are fresh and unique.

3. Dating reignites passion and sparks sexual intimacy. Over time, many couples experience a drift in romance and sexual intimacy. Dating is an opportunity to dress up, make a reservation at a restaurant that doesn't have plastic forks, and linger over dinner. After your date, don't go straight home to tackle laundry, pay bills, and do chores. If you do go home immediately, enjoy each other sexually. For some couples, date night is reserved for sex. That doesn't mean it's going to be boring. In fact, the anticipation can be even better if one of you is a sexual Crock-Pot who takes a little longer to warm up. (If you're a sexual microwave, you don't need the anticipation. You're pretty much always ready.)

4. Dating demonstrates commitment to your marriage. Dating is a signal to children, family, and friends that says, "We're serious about our marriage, and we make a weekly investment in each other." It also says, "Our time together is valuable." One of the greatest gifts you can give your children is prioritizing a weekly date night, because it communicates this message to them: "Mom and Dad love each other and plan on spending time strengthening that love." Investing in your marriage gives your children a sense of security that is desperately needed in young lives. It relieves their fear that Mom and Dad are going to separate like so many other moms and dads they see.

5. Dating gives couples extended periods to destress. It provides the perfect platform for reducing stress and distractions. It's no surprise that one of the biggest killers of marriages is busyness and the breathless pace we keep. (By the way, don't get so busy you skip chapter 4 on slowing down.) Many couples are overextended and underconnected, and an intentional date helps relieve the pressure that sneaks up on marriages.

We would add two more benefits to this list from the University of Virginia.

6. Dating creates anticipation in marriage. We've mentioned anticipating romance and sexual intimacy, but there's more to a date than sex. When you plan a date, you have something on the calendar to look forward to in the grind of life. Dating gets you out of the house and breaks up the weekly routine. Dates that include play, laughter, dreaming, and adventure can keep the power of the ordinary from consuming your marriage.

We've been challenging married couples for many years to go on weekly dates, and not one couple has told us they were disappointed when they accepted our challenge. Actually, the opposite has been true: couples have thanked us for giving them permission to date and encouraging them to do what they know they should have been doing all along.

More than forty years ago, Cathy and I (Jim) decided to make dating each other a weekly, nonnegotiable experience. Then, when Doug and Cathy got married ten years later, we passed on the value of weekly dating to them, and they've eagerly embraced it for more than thirty years. We admit that we've missed a few weeks along the way—but not many.

We've discovered that one of the secrets to the longevity of dating is to always have some ideas of what you and your spouse can do on a future date. Having a list takes away the excuse that "There's nothing to do."

We encourage you to make a list of twenty potential dates you'd like to experience in the next six months. Go ahead and do it right now. Put the book down, get out a sheet of paper or a date journal, and come up with as many date ideas as you can. Return to that list often for inspiration, and continue adding to it.

7. Dating builds memories. When we total up all the dates that Doug and I have shared with our wives over seventy-five combined years (and more), we have a museum filled with experiences and memories. Healthy marriages have happy memories. Let's face it, if you plan to grow old together, there will come a time when the kids move out, and it's just the two of you. You'll have each other, and you'll have your memories.

I (Doug) keep a photo in my office that's close to my heart— it's one of my mom and dad during their engagement. I also have another photo of my parents that was taken a couple weeks before my dad died and left my mom a widow after fifty years of marriage. Here's what I find stunning: my mom had the same expression on her face in both photos—a look of value as she gazed at my dad. That look was apparent fifty years after their engagement because they had spent those years building fun memories.

Fast-forward to a few weeks prior to my mom's death. When she knew she was dying, she told stories of her dates with her Jimmy. She didn't ask to be surrounded with her many bowling trophies. She didn't want to be wrapped up in quilts she had made by hand. And she definitely didn't ask to see a pie chart of her 401(k) retirement account. Instead, she pored over the photos and stories that summed up her life and reminisced about her fifty years of marriage. Marge Fields understood that the most valuable marriage possessions are the shared experiences and fun memories that link a couple's hearts together.

Our lives are a museum of memories that contribute to who we are. Every memory is a frame in the film of life, and each frame adds to our identity and health as human beings. The more positive and frequent the memories, the more powerful the emotional connection.

Several years ago, Cathy and I (Doug) had … um … well … ah … shall we say a romantic rendezvous at a rest stop off the Interstate 5 freeway near San Diego. No need to write any more about our adventure in the car. Let's just say we didn't rest. Now, many years later, whenever we drive to San Diego (which is about ninety miles from our house), one of us just has to say the words "rest stop," and there are immediate smiles. Why? Because that memory was out of the ordinary, spontaneous, fun, and even a bit risky (but not too risky, since it wasn't in the middle of the afternoon). Memories give us a common bond, a shared language, and a deeper connection. When I (Jim) drive by that rest stop, I smile too, but for a different reason. I can't believe Doug just shared that memory with you!

Cathy and I (Jim) have a high-maintenance marriage. We've lasted four decades, but each year hasn't been easy. On our fortieth anniversary, we were sitting on a romantic beach and spontaneously began thinking back on our memorable moments. We reminisced about previous anniversaries, times of romance and travel, and hundreds of weekly dates. As we shared a few of the favorite memories of our life together, it suddenly grew quiet between us. I took Cathy's hands in mine, and looking into her eyes, I said, "I wouldn't change this crazy life together for anything."

She flashed her gorgeous smile and said, "Me neither."

The glue that has held our marriage together is the fun, the dating, and the memories we've collected over the years. All of that has unquestionably outweighed the bad.

We hope you have great memories of fun dates to look back on after decades of marriage. Be courageous enough to make a commitment to start your weekly dates and begin to deepen your marriage with fun and laughter. We promise you'll thank us for challenging you.

QUESTIONS

1. What can you do to inject more fun into your marriage?
2. If you aren't going on a weekly date, discuss a specific day and time to start one. What's holding you back?
3. What changes might you need to make in your schedule and priorities so you can begin emphasizing fun and weekly dates?

Chapter Four

•

SLOW DOWN

Teri and Jason had been married four years, and they were deeply immersed in trying to figure out marriage and family. Teri was pregnant with their second child while their first was still in diapers. Jason was doing well in his job and was focused on climbing the corporate ladder. Teri was trying to do her CPA work from home while her twenty-month-old napped. Throw in their extracurricular activities, and they were running faster than their hearts could handle. They were feeling the pressure that comes with parenting, jobs, chores, marriage, and the blistering pace of life. Bottom line: they were too busy!

When they approached us for help, we found ourselves exhausted just listening to their schedule. You may or may not identify with Jason and Teri's pace, but we'd bet you can recognize the stress that busyness causes. A little later in the chapter, we'll return to this young couple's story and tell you what we told them, but first let's talk about you, your busyness, and the stress it creates in your marriage.

Stress strikes your marriage by targeting and attacking the quality of your communication and the depth of your emotional connection. Stress can cause even good marriages to drift. If you haven't experienced much stress yet, congratulations. But don't get too cocky; it's just a matter of time. Stress is slowly moving toward you. How's that for good news? You've no doubt already discovered that stressful circumstances can arise that aren't your fault. However, most of the time, your own choices and the resulting consequences cause the stress that affects your marriage. Stress happens, but how you choose to deal with it will determine your ability to keep your marriage on course.

BUSY COUPLES CHOOSE BUSY

One of the biggest stressors affecting healthy marriages is the breathless pace at which we choose to live. Busyness isn't innocent; it comes with an expensive price tag.

Friends of ours have been married for only three years, and they recently told us they're pursuing divorce. We were devastated but found their reasoning fascinating: "It wasn't that we stopped loving each other; we were just so distracted and busy that we didn't have the drive to improve our marriage. Our energy has been so focused on our jobs and other activities that our marriage became a casualty [of] our busyness."

It's tragic that they allowed their busyness to distract them from what was most important. They weren't willing to pull out of the fast lane, and that choice crashed their marriage.

Make no mistake about it: busyness is a choice. So much of the drift in marriage points back to the choices couples make. To keep your marriage on a healthy course, headed toward your intended destination, you'll need to make tough choices about the many opportunities that compete for your time. You'll have to choose to say no to important options so you can say yes to what's *most* important.

If you have no time for your marriage, you must shift into crisis mode and make immediate course corrections. You can't just make more time for your marriage. As fun as it would be, it's impossible. All married couples, regardless of income, region, religion, upbringing, and personality, have exactly the same amount of time: 1,440 minutes a day. Yet you have the amazing ability to choose how those precious, fleeting minutes are spent. It's both a privilege and a burden. If you don't learn how to use those minutes to breathe life into your marriage, the drift in your relationship will become apparent.

Although Max Lucado was talking about familiarity and our tendency to lose sight of what's really important, I think this quote applies to busyness as well: "He's an expert in robbing the sparkle and replacing it with the drab .... He won't steal your [marriage] from you; he'll do something far worse. He'll paint it with a familiar coat of drabness .... The poison of [busyness] has deadened your senses to the magic of the moment."[1] That's such a powerful and true statement! Busyness is a thief. It's no wonder that people say, "If the Devil can't make you bad, he will make you busy."

AVOIDING THE CRASH

Several years ago, a big-city commuter train crashed, killing several and seriously injuring hundreds of people. The train was traveling too fast in a location that required it to go slow. When investigators looked into the accident, they identified three factors that contributed to the devastation:

1. A comparable crash had already taken place in a similar location, and the lessons it offered were ignored.
2. The warning lights that informed the conductor to slow down were working, but the driver didn't give it proper attention.
3. The conductor was apparently distracted by his phone.

Sadly, this crash could have been prevented. It's really not all that different from what we experience when we see a marriage crash. Too often, couples

- don't take the time to learn from their past mistakes;
- ignore the warning lights that tell them their marriages are in danger, and
- find other priorities distracting them and preventing them from giving needed attention to their marriages.

To experience a lifelong marriage filled with refreshing time margins and deep intimacy, you must understand the cause of your busyness as well as the consequences. It's easy to simply cast blame on busyness without looking within your own heart to see why you might be so busy. To help me (Jim) escape busyness, I regularly ask myself three questions:

1. Is the pace of my life really sustainable over a long period of time?
2. Do I like the person I'm becoming as a result of the pace I keep?
3. Am I giving Cathy and my family my best during this season?

When I'm busy, the answers to these questions are always no, no, and no! While I'm often tempted to move to a deserted island to escape everything, I'm fully aware that a quick fix isn't a good solution. The long-term answer always tells me to notice the warning lights of busyness, learn from my past mistakes, and make choices that will result in a better, stronger, and healthier Jim.

When I reflect on some of my previous bouts with busyness, I can see that I wasn't willing to make the difficult decisions to unclutter my life so that I could have more time for my primary relationships. The warning lights were working; I just didn't give them the attention they deserved. The warning lights of busyness are fairly obvious. Here are the ones Doug and I have seen in our own lives as well as in the lives of couples we've counseled.

Constant clutter. Rushed lives are often reflected in clutter. For me (Doug), when I'm too busy, it can be seen in my piles. Laundry piles. Paper piles on my desk. Piles in the backyard (thanks to my dog and my not taking the time to remove them). I can create a temporary fix and shove clutter into the closed spaces of my life: filing cabinets, closets, and drawers. But when I'm too busy, I don't need a drawer organizer; I need a drawer exorcist. We're not implying you need to become a neat freak, but we are suggesting that your gathered mess could be making a bigger statement about the pace of your life.

Addiction to speed. This is when you want everything to go faster and faster in your life. You find yourself spending most of your waking moments fueling the adrenaline rush that comes from juggling your many "essential" priorities. You're afraid that if you quit juggling, something is going to crash. Unfortunately, many of those addicted to the speed of life do indeed have something crashing—and it's usually one of their primary relationships.

Extreme multitasking. Do you try to accomplish too many things at once? Can you drive your car on the freeway while shaving your legs or playing bingo on your mobile device? Are you the type who can pay the bills *and* talk on the phone *and* entertain a child *and* make dinner while exercising? If so, it's important to understand that extreme multitasking can cause "inattentional blindness." It won't affect your actual vision, but it does influence your psychological perception of what is most important.

Superficial relationships. Staying on the surface with your spouse and most of the people you know happens because busyness and a hurried life are the enemies of depth. Your life feels as though it's a mile wide and an inch deep, and as a result, you become a shallow person—possibly so shallow that you don't even understand how the pace you keep is affecting your marriage.

Relationship fatigue. Many of these busyness indictors can blend together and sound familiar, but relationship fatigue is when you have very little or no time for the people closest to you. You may not be superficial, but you're too tired, drained, and preoccupied to give time to the people who need and deserve it the most. Instead, they're the ones who get cheated and receive your time scraps.

Spiritual emptiness. Spiritual emptiness can be seen when your desire for worship disappears, your compassion dries up, and you have little, if any, concern for spiritual intimacy with your spouse. The pace of life leaves your soul malnourished, and as a result, you suffer from soul erosion. There is just no time or emotional energy to draw near to God.

If any of these warning lights describe you, please don't stop reading! We realize it could be discouraging if you see yourself in these descriptions. But we're only able to describe you because we've been there *before* you. We've both seen and experienced each of these warning lights. You're not alone, but don't allow our camaraderie to become an excuse for ignoring these signs. Busyness won't simply resolve or disappear on its own. What will disappear is any hope for an abundant life and a joy-filled marriage.

Your answer to busyness won't be found on a deserted island (although a vacation with your spouse might be sweet). To conquer busyness, you have to make *intentional* course corrections. You will find solutions as you dig a little deeper within yourself and ask targeted questions concerning your heart. Like us, you'll most likely find that your answer to busyness isn't improving time efficiency but addressing heart deficiency.

ABUNDANCE OR BUSYNESS

A lot of busyness can signal that you're agreeing to do too much. Saying yes speeds up your life. I (Doug) often find myself saying yes because I desire affirmation and approval. I want someone to say, "Doug, you're so great for volunteering to take on this project." But here's the truth: the project didn't make me busy; my yes did. My heart often chases after the wrong things and leads me to a dead-end street called Busyness.

Jesus said something so appealing to my heart: "The thief comes only to steal and kill and destroy; I have come that [you] may have life, and have it to the full."[2] The New Living Translation says, "My purpose is to give [you] a rich and satisfying life," and the English Standard Version says, "I came that [you] may have life and have it abundantly." Jesus was describing fullness of life. He didn't say, "I came that you might be overwhelmed and busy." Jesus wants to fill your heart with His presence so you won't chase after empty promises that can't ultimately satisfy you. Only He can fix the broken-heart issues that are propelling you toward more busyness.

Jim and I meet with too many couples who have created a script for their marriages that substitutes Jesus's promise of abundance and fullness and replaces it with busyness, activity, and stress. We don't want you to become that kind of couple. We want to help you move from busyness to abundance. You can make practical course corrections to lessen the movement and increase abundance in your marriage. This will require you to do more than just hope things will change. Hope without movement isn't an effective strategy.

Following are three course corrections you can make to move from busyness to abundance in your life and marriage.

1. STRENGTHEN YOUR NO MUSCLE

The little word *yes* is a dirty word that gets you in trouble and adds fuel to your pace. To slow down your life and marriage, you'll need to learn how to say no to really good things so you can say yes to the most important things. I (Doug) am a classic people pleaser who has struggled with feelings of insecurity as long as I can remember. What I know about insecure people is that they want everyone to like and appreciate them. This makes me an expert in saying yes so more people will like me.

Jim and I often laugh that we're both wired in a similar fashion: we want to be the superheroes and save the day. Marital tension often appears when we say yes to others and wind up saying no to our wives as a result. *Yes* is a nasty little word that steals big amounts of time.

Going public and admitting our insecurity instead of keeping it secret has helped us both. When your heart issue is private, it's hiding in the dark. But once you expose it to the light of truth, it can help make your decision-making process much easier. If you try to disguise the real reason you're saying yes so much, you'll continue saying yes. But if you'll admit that something in your heart is broken and is leading you to say yes even when you know it's not healthy for your marriage, that truth will eventually set you free.

One immediate action you can take to combat busyness is to make a list of all the responsibilities you currently have that are causing busyness and stress. Give it some good thought and make sure your list is exhaustive. After you've finished the list, show it to your spouse and allow him or her to add anything you've forgotten or ignored. Then go through the list one responsibility at a time and ask yourself, "If I stop doing this, what will the consequence be?" All of your choices have consequences, and those choices are what have made you so busy.

In another column, write down the consequence next to the responsibility stressor so you can see what you're dealing with. After that column is complete, start crossing responsibilities off your list. It will feel painful at first because you'll be personalizing the corresponding consequences (even though nothing has happened yet). Be honest enough with yourself to admit that if you can't find a responsibility to cross off the list, you may be more broken than you realize. You can't do everything! Remember, you have only 1,440 minutes a day. You can't be all things to all people. There is a Messiah, but you're not Him. Here's the good news, though: you can talk to Jesus and ask Him to give you both the wisdom and discernment to make better choices.

At the beginning of this chapter, we told you about Teri and Jason, the couple who felt overwhelmed trying to juggle everything they said yes to. When they came to see us, we assigned them this exercise, and after they listed all the responsibilities and consequences they could think of, we said, "We want you to cross off five things from this list before you leave our office. To make it a little easier on you, we're going to quantify it by saying this is only a six-month experiment. You don't have to say no forever—just right now and only for six months. So start cutting."

They both rolled their eyes, and Teri immediately said, "You don't understand our world."

Jim and I were tempted to laugh in their faces, but we held it together. Then Teri and Jason used the classic line people use when they're so overwhelmed they can't see any realistic escape: "We can't cut anything out right now."

At that point, I (Jim) gave them one of my go-to counseling lines: "Okay, that's your choice. You may not be ready right now, but when the pain of remaining the same is greater than the pain of changing, you'll change."

They left our office without cutting a single responsibility. Honestly, Doug and I didn't hold out much hope that they would make the difficult decisions needed to ignite the changes they longed for in their lives and marriage. However, we were happily proved wrong when we received an email from them a few months later. Here's an excerpt:

> We reluctantly decided to make some changes to our pace of life. No, we didn't move to Hawaii. We were just so tired of being tired, and nothing seemed to be working to slow us down. You could say that the pain of staying the same got too great, Jim (wink). Change had to be easier. We decided to take your cutting challenge seriously. We settled down at the kitchen table with pen and paper, our calendar, a cup of coffee for Jason, [and] a glass of wine (or two) for me, and we began the surgery of removing the yeses from our lives. We talked

about everything we were doing and left no stone unturned. We were desperate to make the changes before our baby arrived. We decided to cut back some hours at work [that] would put the goal of buying a house off for two years. We made decisions that cost us financially but were costing us more in stress. We realized that we could actually delay some gratification in order to have more "us" time. As much as Jason loves playing basketball, two nights a week were painfully carved to one.

Bottom line: we purged a lot of commitments [on our] list that previously seemed impossible to cut. [It was] painful at first, but now, months later, life is so much better. What appeared to be excruciating hasn't [proved] to be rough at all. We're learning to develop our no muscle[s]. When Jason heads to work in the morning, we'll kiss and say, "Have a great day saying no to more." We laugh, but only because it's true. It is fun to say no because we know it's not fun to live out what the yes brings.

Our priorities have slowly shifted, and we've joined a small group at church with friends who have been holding us accountable [for] our choices. It's a great group of people our age who understand busyness and stress. Anyway, we just wanted you to know that when we left your offices, we thought you were both so out of touch with real couples. We were wrong, and you were right (doesn't that feel good to hear?). Your advice is working, and we're thankful! Gotta go. The baby is crying.

We're so glad Teri and Jason were courageous enough to say no so they could say yes to more for their marriage.

2. SAY NO TO NOISE

There are lots of different types of noise that clutter our minds and busy our lives. The question for you to ponder in your own life is, What do you consider noise? We view noise as anything that distracts us from intimacy, listening, and reflecting.

One noise that is especially obnoxious is what I (Doug) call mobile-phone noise. It's always calling my name. It's fun noise, and I actually like it a lot—too much, in fact, and that's the problem. It was stealing my attention from those who were closest to me. Because of that, I now have a self-imposed, self-regulated rule about answering my phone when Cathy or any of my kids are in the car with me. I just let it ring until it switches to voice mail. I don't want that noise competing with those I love the most. This policy has been in place for many years, and I've never regretted missing a call. I love the time with my loved ones when we're in the car. They're my captive audience. We're all trapped together with no interruptions. The car is a great place for communication to occur naturally.

It might be a new concept for you to think about your mobile device as noise, but consider this: one study revealed that the average time spent answering a text message is less than thirty seconds, and the average person looks at his or her handheld device eighty-five times a day.[3] These noisy intruders enter our lives uninvited and distract us from relationships. They can even wound those we love. For example, when you look at a text message while you're with your spouse, you interrupt a relational connection. By simply glancing at the text while you're engaged in conversation, it can send the message, "This phone is more important to me than you are."

Technoference is a word used to describe technology interfering with relationships. We see this all the time when couples are sitting in a restaurant knee to knee but not eye to eye. It's the new normal. They're physically close yet emotionally distant and disconnected because they're looking at their devices. Relationship experts would even argue that our smartphones are making us *stupid* in relationships.

At this point you may be thinking, *What does this have to do with busyness and the long-term success of my marriage?* Everything! All those intruding noises are competing for those finite 1,440 minutes you own each day. The trade-off for spending some of those minutes texting or using social media isn't worth the sacrificed intimacy when you could be spending that time with your spouse. Your focused presence with your spouse is a sign of caring and connectedness. To prevent marriage drift, you must take advantage of opportunities for connection and put the phone down. That text, game, or photo can wait.

It's not uncommon for couples to establish a few noise-reducing rules for their marriage, and we would challenge you to come up with some that work for you. I (Doug) have friends who put their phones in "media jail" for all their meals and turn them off at 8:00 p.m. In addition to my no-phone-while-my-family-is-in-the-car rule, Cathy and I have a rule that we don't look at our phones when we're in bed. Our bed is a sacred place, and not just for sex. It's for conversation, snuggling, prayer, and laughter. In other words, connection. We don't need the added noise competing for those precious minutes, and neither do you.

Here are two important words that may help you: *power button.* It's okay to disconnect from your devices so you and your spouse can connect. Come up with a plan and put it into action to minimize tech distractions. We're not asking you to get rid of your smartphone and become Amish, buy a buggy, and escape all electronics. But we know that a less hurried and interrupted life requires some silence, and that silence isn't native to our world. If you're going to find silence, you'll have to pursue it, and saying no to your mobile device more often will definitely help.

3. PRACTICE THE 1 PERCENT RULE

In chapter 3, we introduced the idea of a weekly date consisting of one hour and forty minutes or 1 percent of the 1,440 minutes you have at your disposal. What if you set aside 1 percent of your time *each day* for your spouse? That's only fourteen minutes and forty seconds per day, so let's round up and make it fifteen minutes.

Start with giving your spouse just 1 percent of your day. That's fifteen minutes of face-to-face, knee-to-knee connection. This means turning off the television, shutting down the computer, and putting your phone in jail. These few minutes, set aside every day, will make a big difference over the course of weeks, months, years, and decades. Your marriage can become rock solid if you slow things down, block out noise, and commit to a daily time together. Most of us pack too much into those 1,440 minutes a week, and it leaves us harried, stressed, and lacking intimacy with our spouses. Let's change that! Fifteen minutes isn't much, and we know you can do this!

Our dear friends Fadi and Kim actually give each other at least thirty minutes a day. Every morning before work, they sit down together with cups of coffee and have an intentional time of connecting with each other. They'll often end that morning time with a prayer, a hug, and a kiss. Then they go their separate ways and run a business, chauffeur four kids, ride horses, work on their house, entertain friends, do homework with the kids, and much more. You get the drill. When things begin to settle down at night, they sit for fifteen minutes and each have a glass of wine together to close out the day. Fadi calls this routine their "beverage bookends" (coffee in the morning and wine in the evening).

Do they share other times throughout the day? Sure, but their bookend moments are intentional and protected: the phone goes unanswered, and their children know not to interrupt them. Fadi and Kim—and others with strong, healthy marriages—know the importance of these focused times together and make them happen so their marriage doesn't drift. It doesn't have to be a lot of time for it to be a powerful time.

There's a great story in the Bible where Jesus challenged a woman named Martha to slow down and focus on what mattered most. He essentially told her that her busyness was quenching her chance at abundance.[4] That's our message to you: if you want to win in marriage, you have to figure out how to slow down, pay attention to what's in your heart that's causing you to hurry, and learn to say no to the intruding noises and priorities that are stealing some of those precious 1,440 minutes from you.

Busyness doesn't have to define you or your marriage. In marriage you're called to …

> love, not race;
> serve, not rush; and
> care, not hurry.

True love requires time, and time is something busy people don't have. Allow your love to stop, stroll, and even meander. That type of love will defeat busyness, win over stress, and keep you headed toward your intended destination.

QUESTIONS

1. What kind of "noise" is potentially affecting your relationship with your spouse?
2. Are you already applying the 1 percent rule of spending fifteen minutes a day sitting together, relaxing, and connecting? If not, what needs to change so you can implement this rule?
3. What are some deliberate ways you can eliminate phone noise for a specific period of time each day to enhance your relationship?

Chapter Five

•

CELEBRATE DIFFERENCES

Do you ever feel you married someone very different from you? If so, you're not alone. The famous actress Katharine Hepburn once said, "Sometimes I wonder if men and women really suit each other. Perhaps they should live next door and just visit now and then." It's a funny line, but we sort of understand it. When John Gray published the best-selling book *Men Are from Mars, Women Are from Venus,* we bought it, partly because the title clearly summarized our research. More times than we can count, we've actually thought our spouses act as if they're from different planets, and we're 100 percent confident they'd say the same about us.

Many couples believe that the fewer differences they have with their spouses, the better their marriages will be. While that might be true with some marriages, it's not necessarily a truism. The key factor isn't how different your spouse is from you but how you choose to handle your differences.

ATTRACT AND ATTACK

You've probably heard this famous cliché: before marriage, differences *attract*; after marriage, differences *attack*. It's more than a cliché. There's a lot of truth to that statement. Before Cathy and I (Doug) married, we saw each other's differences as cute and endearing. After we married, when we were living in the same house and sharing the same bed, those same differences lost their cuteness and started to bug each of us. We're different in a lot of unique ways: communication styles, likes and dislikes, temperaments, personalities, recreation choices, food choices, and so on. For example:

Doug	Cathy
Personality: extrovert	Personality: introvert
Temperament: intense/emotional	Temperament: kicked back/ relaxed
Movie likes: action/comedy	Movie likes: romance/Hallmark classics
Recreation: CrossFit, competition, intense workout	Recreation: relaxing walk with a friend
Showing love: with words	Showing love: through presence

Did you marry someone different from you? For Cathy and me, once the infatuation over our uniqueness wore off—as it does in every marriage—we had to stare our differences directly in the face. Honestly, it was a little frightening. Now, with more than thirty years of marriage under our belts and some wisdom that comes with age and experience, I can clearly see that a big part of being bugged had to do with my immaturity and inability to fully appreciate

Cathy's differences. In my sophomoric approach, I wanted her to be a photocopy of me instead of celebrating the fact that God had designed her to be an original masterpiece. How I wish I could have some of those early years back to fully recognize and appreciate those differences.

Many factors make you and your spouse unique: upbringings, heredity, worldviews, distinctive desires, biology, and even male-and-female differences. The couples who learn to accept and celebrate these differences are the most effective at making marriage work. They come to understand that different isn't better or worse; it's just ... different.

WHY DO YOU WANT TO CHANGE YOUR SPOUSE?

Your differences define you. They make you uniquely and wonderfully you. When your spouse isn't like you, the answer isn't to initiate Operation Change My Spouse. The longer you live with the fantasy of thinking you can transform anyone other than yourself, the more miserable you'll be. As we mentioned in chapter 2, if you keep trying to change your spouse, you'll continually be disappointed. If you've been spending this first season of your marriage trying to make your spouse more like you, our guess is that it's not working out very well.

Why do you think so many spouses keep trying to make their partner more like themselves when the odds of change are so low? This is such an important question that we focus on it in both premarital and postmarital counseling. Let's get deep for a minute:

Could it be that your attempts to change your spouse are rooted in your own brokenness or insecurities? Or maybe they're fueled by your selfishness and self-centeredness. Could it be that your pride is causing you to believe that your way, style, and actions are *right*, and your spouse's are *wrong*?

Regardless of your reasons for trying to change your spouse, the only modification you'll find successful is working on your own stuff and not your spouse's. You'll struggle in your marriage if you keep trying to get your spouse to think and act like you. That shouldn't be your ultimate goal. It's been said that the goal of marriage is not to think alike but to think together. That is so good! But we realize it's a lot easier said than done. So what can we do?

LEARNING TO APPRECIATE YOUR DIFFERENCES

As I (Doug) highlighted earlier, I'm extroverted, and Cathy is introverted. When we first got married, we would go out with friends or be invited to parties. As an extrovert, I was excited, and it didn't take me long to meet everyone in the room. I'd easily move from person to person, having superficial conversations that fueled my energy tank (classic extrovert). Those types of interactions drained Cathy. She was happy to attend social functions, but once we got there, the differences in how we socialized were like night and day (or Mars and Venus). She didn't move around the room and schmooze with ease. She usually wound up spending the whole night talking with one or two people in a quieter location. Blah! Can you say boring? To me, that wasn't how to be at a social event.

On our drive home, I'd ask, "What was wrong with you tonight?"

Caught off guard, Cathy would say, "What do you mean?"

I'd quickly reply, "Well, it didn't look like you were having much fun. You didn't meet most of the people there." In my immaturity, I was really thinking, *How rude of you not to meet everyone like I did.* Then my insecurity would bubble up, and I'd think, *If she would be just a little friendlier, she would be a better reflection of me.* Yikes! In other words, *If you talk more, people might think you're friendlier, and that would make me look better.*

I know what you're thinking: *What an insecure, selfish jerk!* You're right. I wanted to pull her away from the wall into my active, extroverted arena and show off my dance partner. But she wanted to dance to her own style of music. I hate to admit this, but earlier in our marriage, I was 100 percent confident that my style was the right style and Cathy would be happier if she were more extroverted like me. I'm sure I viewed introversion as a character flaw. Again, I know, what a jerk!

When you try to make your spouse more like you, it sends a message titled "Rejection." You may not verbally say, "I reject you," but what your spouse hears is, "I reject your personality, your individuality, and basically how God created you. I don't like you for who you are." When your spouse feels rejected, his or her heart pulls away from you.

Here's a helpful marriage principle to remember: *the heart is repelled from that which rejects it.* If you've been dropping hints that your spouse should change, or shaming your spouse for not being more like you, or being passive-aggressive when your spouse does something in a different way than you'd do it, that's rejection. You're rejecting the very person you're intended to love more deeply than any other human.

If this describes you, you're magnifying the drift in your marriage. Your spouse may be pulling away from you because he or she feels the sting of your rejection. Again, the heart is repelled from that which rejects it. You may view your actions as coaching or helping or guiding your spouse to be a better person (which usually means more like you), but it's still rejection. In addition to apologizing for trying to change your spouse, you need to move from a posture of *rejection* to actions of *respect*.

RESPECTING DIFFERENCES LEADS TO EMBRACING THEM

Fast-forward to today. Cathy would testify that I (Doug) now have a vastly different understanding and appreciation of her differences. Guess what? She didn't change at all. I did. I made the very necessary course corrections. When I realized that I was damaging her heart by trying to get her to be more like me, I confessed my selfishness and immaturity and begged her for forgiveness. I came to better understand that we're divinely designed to be different.

This may sound odd to you after what I've just written, but I came to realize that I wanted to be more like Cathy. She has so many amazing qualities that have emerged from her unique personality. She has a calmness that is so attractive to me. She cares deeply for people and doesn't rush off to the next conversation like I tend to do. Her pace of life is slower than mine, and I'm drawn to her "chill" attitude. She rarely gets bent out of shape. She knows Jesus and walks with

Him daily, and she's secure in her identity as a child of God. Even as I write this, I'm blown away by how amazing she is, and I'm equally blown away by how stupid I was during our early years of marriage when I tried to make her more like me. Argh! So embarrassing.

A NEW VIEW

If you want to build your marriage on a solid foundation—and we think you do, since you're still reading—you may need to beg God to help you change your perspective. This specific course correction needs to include a change in the way you see your spouse. What if you began to view your spouse's differences as strengths instead of weaknesses? Consider asking yourself, "What if I really believed our heavenly Father crafted the specific characteristics infused in my spouse's DNA?"

Think about it: What if the quality you want to change in your spouse was actually God's dream and design for him or her from the very beginning? Imagine Jesus saying these words about your spouse:

> I love _____ so much, and I'm thrilled with the way I created him/her. _____ is My original masterpiece, and I'm so excited for _____ to come alive and become all I've created him/her to be. Believe Me, when _____ becomes who I've designed him/her to be, you'll be so amazed. Your job as husband/wife is to nurture _____'s uniqueness and help _____ achieve My

design for him/her. Then you'll see exactly why I
created _____ in that unique way. Oh,
by the way, I love you deeply too, and I want you
to become uniquely you, the person I created you
to be. When you are both uniquely you, so much
abundance will come your way.

You may need to reread this a few times so the power behind
those words will begin to sink into your soul and give you a new
appreciation for your spouse.

LOVE AND RESPECT

Embracing your spouse's differences affords you the greatest
opportunity to communicate unconditional love. Unconditional
love—feeling loved without conditions—is the true longing of
every heart. To be known and loved for who you are—no matter
what—is a relationship miracle. It's the desire of your heart whether
or not you'd explain it that way. It's the way God loves you, and it's
how you were created to love and be loved. In one simple sentence,
Scripture sheds light on how to communicate love in spite of our
differences: "Each [man] must love his wife as he loves himself, and
the wife must respect her husband."[1]

We believe this verse contains the key to developing a healthy
relationship and keeping the spark burning bright in your marriage. These words suggest that one of the greatest needs a woman
has is to experience *love* from her husband. Likewise, one of the
greatest relational needs a man has is to experience *respect* from

his wife. If a woman doesn't feel intentional love from her husband—pursuing her, being generous with words of affection and adoration, showing small and big acts of love and service—she'll wilt like an unwatered flower. If a man doesn't feel that his wife respects, values, and admires him, he will disengage and drift from the relationship. Love for a woman and respect for a man are like oxygen and water for a plant, essential ingredients that keep the marriage fires burning.

Author Emerson Eggerichs brought this biblical concept to the forefront of the marriage conversation in his best-selling book *Love and Respect*. He wrote, "A husband is even called to love a disrespectful wife, and a wife is called to respect an unloving husband."[2] That's a big challenge!

Let's consider this love-respect idea in light of your differences. One of the greatest opportunities you have to communicate love and respect in your marriage is in the midst of your differences. Just like other differences between you and your spouse, you'll ask each other different questions.

If you're the wife, your husband wants to know, "Despite my differences and failings, do you respect me?"

His heart needs you to say, "Yes, I respect you even though I know your imperfections and the fact that you're so different from me." When you respond to your husband this way, you're expressing unconditional love. This doesn't mean you worship him as if he can do no wrong; it simply means that in the midst of your differences, you fuel his heart through your expression of respect. Your respect for him will draw him closer to you with a deeper love and a stronger commitment to your marriage. When you say yes to respect, you're loving your husband without condition, and that's incredibly powerful.

It's important to be the source of the highest level of respect in your husband's life. If your respect level is low and he finds a higher level of respect from other women in his world (e.g., at work, in the neighborhood, at the gym, on Facebook, etc.), there becomes a real risk of trouble in your marriage. No one should respect your husband more than you. When you show him respect, we think you'll see a difference you'll appreciate.

All right, men, let's consider your wife's question. She's not asking, "Do you respect me?" Her question is very clear: "Do you love, adore, and value me?" Imagine your wife waking up every day wanting you to answer that question.

When Cathy and I (Jim) were first married, she would ask me all the time, "Do you love me?" To be honest, it kind of bugged me. Of course I loved her. I couldn't figure out what I was doing wrong that made her always want reassurance. It made me think of the old, grouchy husband who said to his wife, "I told you on our wedding day, 'I love you,' and if I change my mind, I'll tell you!" I was young in marriage, but I was old enough to know that would be a dumb thing to say.

I slowly realized that Cathy's heart and mind needed frequent reassurance of my love for her. I didn't need the same reassurance from her; I never questioned her love for me. But I often wondered, despite our differences, if she respected me.

When I really began to understand that Cathy and I communicate love differently, I became much more understanding and tried to communicate more often and more clearly that I indeed loved her.

The key principle here is this: *how you communicate love to your spouse could be different from how you need to receive and feel it.*

Your wife is asking, "Do you love and value me despite our differences? Am I valuable enough to catch your eye, to hold your attention, to capture your heart? Am I the one?" She isn't wondering whether she made your top-five list. She wants to know if you value her more than any other person on Earth. When a woman experiences that type of love, she'll feel emotionally secure and safe with the man she desperately wants to respect.

Let's apply this principle to a real-life scenario. Let's say I (Doug) come home with some good news about a speaking request that will pay for Cathy and me to go to Hawaii and stay for a few days after the event. I'm thrilled. It seems like a no-brainer yes opportunity. (If I'm getting a paid speaking gig in Hawaii, I don't even need to pray about it!) But in my excitement, I don't take our differences into consideration or think about how best to love Cathy as I share *my* good news.

Here's how it played out: I got home, bolted through the door, and shouted, "We're going to Hawaii! Woo-hoo!" I expected Cathy to respond with the same enthusiasm and maybe even a little affirmation of her respect for me. My heart would have been happy to hear, "Yes! Wow, Doug, you're my hero! I respect you so much for how you make life better for me and the kids."

Uh, well, let's just say that didn't happen. Instead, Cathy raised several legitimate questions: "How can we afford it?" "Who will take care of the kids?" "What will we do with the house?"

While that wasn't the response I had envisioned, it wasn't Cathy's fault. Our differences simply collided. I knew the speaking engagement was a year away, and being a futurist and a dreamer, I was excited to be the messenger of this wonderful news. At that time, Cathy was deep in mom mode, and the prospect of this kind of trip seemed more like a burden for her than a vacation. She was an overwhelmed mom who was living in the reality of the here and now. She wasn't dreaming about the future with me. She was trying to get through the evening with dinner, dishes, baths, laundry, and whatever else was on her to-do list.

My mistake was not understanding how she would receive my great news. I thought *Hawaii* would be the magic word, and instead, she focused on the word *going* and all that would entail for a busy mom. If I had been more aware of our differences, I would have tempered my enthusiasm and said, "Hey, babe, in about a year, we have an opportunity to go to a place we've dreamed of going—Hawaii! I'd love to spend a week there with you, and I just received a speaking request that will make this happen. They're going to pay for it all *and* pay me to speak. Even though it's a year away, I've asked your mom if she would watch the kids, and she was thrilled. We don't need to decide today, but I would sure love to get away with you." If I had made this wise move, it would have shown Cathy that I valued her and honored our differences.

It's in real-life, everyday marriage that our differences come into play. The differences you have with your spouse can pull you apart and speed up the marriage drift, or they can open a door of opportunity to course-correct and love your spouse unconditionally. A big part of having good communication with your spouse is learning to speak the language he or she hears most clearly.

SPEAKING YOUR SPOUSE'S LOVE LANGUAGE

Dr. Gary Chapman has been a mentor to us for years, and in his best-selling book *The 5 Love Languages*, he powerfully observes that when a couple learns each other's unique love language and becomes proficient in speaking it, the relationship will thrive. This is one of your jobs on this marital journey. If you don't know your spouse's love language, you may be trying your best to communicate love to your spouse but not connecting as effectively as you'd like. It may seem to your spouse that you're speaking a foreign language. Let's look briefly at Chapman's five love languages.[3]

1. Words of affirmation. If your spouse's primary love language is affirmation, words of encouragement, praise, and compliments scream *love* to him or her. Mark Twain once said, "I can live for two months on a good compliment." This statement proves that words of affirmation weren't Twain's primary love language. If this is your spouse's top love language, he or she needs words of affirmation on a daily basis.

This is my (Doug's) primary love language, and I feel most connected to Cathy when she uses words to breathe life into me. But because words aren't her primary love language, they don't come naturally to her. I can use positive words all day long. It's easy to be encouraging: I'm a natural at it because it's my love language. The flip side is that negative or critical words sting me more deeply than they do Cathy. Even though this isn't her love language, she has learned how to love me with words.

2. Acts of service. If this is your spouse's primary love language, actions communicate love most strongly to him or her. Actions speak much louder than words and even drown them out. Hearing the phrase "Let me do that for you" is music to your spouse's ears. He or she feels love when you notice something that needs to be done and do it. It might seem like a simple chore to you, but it's an extreme expression of love to your spouse. The downside is that broken promises or laziness can hurt your spouse more deeply and make him or her feel unloved.

3. Physical touch. Nothing conveys love more deeply than warm, appropriate touch if this is your spouse's love language. It's not just about physical intimacy in the bedroom; it's about everyday physical connections like hugging, hand-holding, and kissing. Physical contact makes your spouse come alive. The more affection, the better. If you withhold physical expressions of love from your spouse, it's like withholding water from a thirsty traveler crawling across a hot desert. For your spouse, touch is life.

4. Receiving gifts. If a tangible gift conveys love to your spouse, this is his or her primary love language. Needing you to express love this way isn't materialistic or selfish. For your spouse, it's not as much about the gift as it is the thought behind it. The gift reflects appreciation and thoughtfulness. It doesn't have to be extravagant or elaborate as long as it's meaningful and thoughtful. If you give your spouse an impersonal gift or forget a gift for a special occasion, he or she may feel rejected.

5. Quality time. If this is your spouse's primary love language, he or she craves your undivided attention. Your spouse feels best loved when he or she is with you. Whether it's a quiet dinner or an afternoon walk, spending time with you makes him or her feel more love, satisfaction, and comfort than anything else. If quality time conveys love to your spouse, he or she may feel hurt if you don't listen or aren't physically present. Your spouse may view breaking a date, blowing off a planned time together, or always checking your phone as a devastating betrayal.

After reading these short descriptions, do you think you know your spouse's primary love language? What about your own? Our guess is that you and your spouse probably have different love languages and will need to learn each other's language and practice speaking it until you become fluent and comfortable.

All five of the love languages are important, but it's imperative to know your spouse's primary love language and liberally speak it. Like Doug, my (Jim's) love language is words of affirmation, and Cathy's is acts of service. When Cathy compliments me or uses kind, thoughtful words, it's as if she's reaching deep into my heart and turning the love meter on high. Words are so powerful for me that I've kept her encouraging love notes from years ago.

Though Cathy also appreciates words of affirmation, she doesn't feel them or need them as deeply as I do. But when I fold the laundry or clean up the kitchen, she feels valued and receives those actions as love. If I'm being honest, I'd be a better husband if her love language was words of affirmation! Instead, to serve her most powerfully, I have to do what feels unnatural to me. It was a big aha moment when I realized that we express and receive love differently. When I made a concentrated effort to learn Cathy's love language and speak it, it improved our relationship immediately.

It's so simple to win in marriage when you discover and learn to speak your spouse's primary love language. Chances are really good that you married someone who appreciates the other four love languages but comes alive and feels loved at a much deeper level when you speak his or her primary love language and become an expert at it.[4]

DIFFERENT ROLES AND RESPONSIBILITIES

Learning each other's primary love language can be a fun and enlightening experience that highlights your differences but also gives you an opportunity to love one another in a way that will make you both come alive. Unfortunately, we can't end this chapter without discussing a topic that's not so fun: chores (better known as roles and responsibilities). What happens in marriage when roles and responsibilities collide with our differences? This issue may have been discussed in your premarital counseling sessions, but we've found that most newly married couples don't really understand the concept of roles and responsibilities until the first few years of marriage. Bottom line: couples who share roles and responsibilities are happier. If only it were that simple!

I (Jim) remember having a wonderful conversation about this with a couple who was reading through our *Getting Ready for Marriage* book and workbook. The young woman told me, "We adore each other's differences, and we don't think we'll have any issues sharing all the roles and responsibilities."

I smiled and asked, "Okay, but have you thought about the logistics of who does what?"

The couple met my question with a "We're so in love with each other that nothing will cause us to drift" look. Then the young man said, "No, but we'll work it out."

When I met with this couple for their six-month postmarriage checkup appointment, I discovered that their biggest struggle was navigating their very different expectations over who did what. Hmm! I acted shocked.

She expected her new husband to share the cooking and cleaning duties, but he came from a family where his mom did all the kitchen work, and he assumed his wife would perform those tasks. Their current differences and conflicts stemmed from the way they were brought up and the expectations they brought into their marriage. After only six months, they were experiencing the pain and anger of unfulfilled and unrealistic expectations. The wife was extremely frustrated and harbored resentment toward her husband because she felt as if she was working a second shift when she got home from her job, while her husband played video games to relax after his long day at work. This was a disaster waiting to happen. I'm glad they kept their checkup appointment, and I'm confident they'll make the necessary course corrections with more defined, realistic, and shared expectations.

According to *The Couple Checkup*, healthy couples typically view their roles in the following five ways. As you look over this list taken from the book, think about whether these qualities are currently true of your marriage.

> 1. Both are equally willing to make adjustments in their marriage.

2. Both work hard to have an equal relationship.
[*Equal* doesn't have to mean "same."]

3. Both are satisfied with [the] division of housework.

4. The couple makes most decisions jointly.

5. Household tasks are divided based on preferences, not tradition.[5]

If you're struggling with differences in how you view your current roles and responsibilities in marriage, we suggest you make a list of them and define each one. Be as specific as possible about who will do what and when and how. Even if you think you have a good grasp on your current situation, it wouldn't hurt to reevaluate your roles and responsibilities biannually to discuss how you feel about your present situation and ensure there isn't any low-level, lingering anger and resentment.

Beside each role and responsibility, place one of these letters: B (both), M (me), or S (spouse). Once you've divided and agreed to these roles and responsibilities, don't look over your spouse's shoulder to make sure that he or she is performing the tasks *as you would*. Allow your spouse the freedom to approach these responsibilities differently. For example, Cathy prefers that I (Jim) leave the kitchen while she's cooking, but after dinner, when I take over to wash the dishes, I don't care if she's in the kitchen. She cares about her cooking time, and I've had to learn to honor her preferences. We've found that the divide-and-conquer technique works best for us (i.e., while she cooks, I do something else), but if you have a controlling or perfectionist personality, you may struggle letting go and allowing your spouse to handle the task. (We'll probably see you in our counseling office pretty soon. Controlling, perfectionist people tend to spend a lot of money on therapy.)

As you make your "Who is going to do what?" list, you can rest assured that those roles and responsibilities will morph over the course of your marriage. It's okay to change things up occasionally and swap roles with your spouse.

My (Doug's) dad was an accountant, which meant he paid the bills and balanced the checkbook in the marriage. When Cathy and I were first married, I embraced that role, and Cathy was absolutely fine with it, since her dad also handled the family finances. But about ten years into our marriage, I was under tremendous stress with book deadlines, and it seemed as if I was writing all the time. Cathy graciously asked if there was anything she could do to help me until the book was completed. I asked, "Do you think you could go through that stack of bills and pay them before they shut off all our utilities?" Guess what? Twenty-plus years later, she's still paying the bills and actually does a much better job than I ever did. (Sorry, accountant dad!)

Don't ever think you're stuck with a responsibility throughout your entire marriage. Experiment with changing roles, and be sure to extend grace to each other. If you do make changes, please be sure you don't switch things up in anger or revenge (e.g., "Okay, so your shirts don't look as nice as you want them? Why don't you do laundry from now on?"). The goal of switching roles should be experimentation or serving each other, not to punish your partner.

As Jim and I look back on our marriages, we have to laugh at how we approached differences with our spouses during the first few years versus how we approach those differences now. For some reason, both of us were intent on changing our wives and making them more like us so they could be much happier. What a joke! It didn't work for either of us, and it won't work for you. For the most part, those differences are still there. Cathy Fields still squeezes the toothpaste tube from the middle, and Cathy Burns is still late for church every week! We were the ones who changed. We had to learn that most of our differences really don't matter and certainly aren't worth fighting over.

Wisdom can grow in your life as you learn from your mistakes. Embrace as many differences as you possibly can, and you might just realize (like we did) that a happy marriage doesn't sweat the small stuff—and most everything is small stuff.

QUESTIONS

1. What first attracted you to your spouse and then began to bug you? How are you doing with that difference now?
2. What makes respecting differences, or even embracing them, difficult for you to do?
3. Which of the differences between you and your spouse do you especially appreciate?

Chapter Six

•

CHOOSE THE POSITIVE

I (Doug) used to believe I was a really good singer. I actually like to sing, but I really only know three songs—and in the interest of total disclosure, I only know a few lines from each one. But that reality doesn't stop me from regularly "blessing" my family with my unique renditions of the original songs. My limited repertoire includes "When a Man Loves a Woman" (usually sung as I'm walking in the door when I know Cathy is home), "God Rest Ye Merry Gentlemen" (during the months of November and December), and "Humble Thyself in the Sight of the Lord" (when I'm in praise mode).

I can actually play "Humble Thyself" on the guitar because it requires only two chords (D and E minor), but I've been told, "Stick to speaking and writing because you'll never be good at leading singing, since it's obvious you're tone deaf!" Not what any aspiring singer wants to hear … but it's true. Even my wife has tenderly asked me a few times to sing quietly at church because my voice has the unique ability to move her immediately from praise to pain. When it comes to music, I am genuinely tone deaf.

A lot of marriages are tone deaf too. Many couples can't hear the negative tone that accompanies their communication. As you've probably learned by now in your own marriage, it's not always *what* you say to each other that creates tension; it's *how* you say it. The how involves *tone*. Thankfully, unlike my singing, positive tones and healthy communication are learned traits. I could spend millions of dollars on voice lessons, but I'll most likely still be tone deaf. I can't change that condition. But you can learn to change the tone in your marriage and begin to make beautiful music together. This change isn't always easy, but we're going to show you how a more positive tone can bring about big changes—and we'll even help you begin to flex those optimism muscles.

Before we get too far into this chapter, we want to let you know that we fully understand it's not always *how* you say something; it can also be *what* you say that creates conflict and hurt feelings.

We have a good friend whose tone is usually very energetic and upbeat—really, he's a very optimistic guy. One day his wife came out of the bedroom after dressing up for their dinner date and asked him a simple question: "How do my new white pants look?" She spun around in eager anticipation of a glowing compliment.

He met her twirl with an enthusiastic smile and said, "Honey, they look great! I like them a lot. They don't make your butt look so big."

She slammed the brakes on her spin, looked directly at him, and snarled, "Try that again."

Mr. Positive quickly realized his poor word choice, panicked, and tried to fix it by saying, "No, honey, I mean it. The pants are great. What I was trying to say is that they just don't make your butt look as big as it actually is!"

Our buddy was positive, peppy, and pretty stupid. Occasionally it's *what* you say that gets you in trouble. By the way, Mr. Positive told us that sleeping on the couch that night wasn't as comfortable as snuggling with his wife and her *perfect* figure.

Now back to tone.

WE FEEL TONE STRONGER THAN WE HEAR WORDS

When negative words are combined with negative tone, trouble is bound to follow. In fact, it's double the trouble. When you express your words with a tone of

> sarcasm,
> shame,
> pessimism,
> insincerity,
> guilt,
> negativity,
> assumption, or
> speculation,

your spouse barely hears the actual words, but the tone shouts at her loud and clear. So many times in both of our marriages, we remember the location where an argument took place but can't remember the specific topic. Can you relate? Our bet is that you've had a conflict that was less about the words and more about the negative energy behind the words. Why? Because we tend to feel tone stronger than the words we hear.

As I mentioned earlier, my (Jim's) wife, Cathy, has been known to be late. Okay, the truth is she's late a lot! Over the years I've learned to manage my tongue (most of the time), but even when I'm silent or speechless, an exasperated sigh can reveal my negativity. Or when we're getting into the car and I know we're going to be late, I can simply take a heavy, deep breath that she receives as a tone of disappointment. To Cathy, it doesn't matter: even when I don't use any words, she can hear my frustration clearly.

Here's the truth about your spouse: you didn't marry a robot. Robots don't discern tone; they simply respond to words. Our phones' operating systems (Siri on my iPhone) aren't smart enough to pick up on tone or innuendo. But our spouses pick up on it quickly. You married an amazing person who is wise and emotionally aware enough to discern your tone and interpret it when it's negative. A negative tone can create unnecessary defensiveness and stir up additional conflict. A lot of the time, the issue that created the tension wasn't what escalated it. The conflict began as a miniflame until the negative tone added fuel, and it combusted into a blazing inferno. A little negativity can create a lot of damage.

Once a spouse hears a negative, demeaning tone, all the good stuff in his or her brain stops working the way it should. It produces a chemical reaction of stress hormones that simultaneously shut down good communication and intimacy. If you regularly use a negative tone with your spouse, you might be reading all this and thinking, *Well, when I'm really mad, I can't control my tone.* While that statement may feel 100 percent accurate, it's 100 percent wrong. *Tone isn't a matter of self-control; it's a matter of choice.*

The majority of the time, we're in control of our tone when we're talking with friends, when we're at work, and even when we're engaging with total strangers. Negative tone tends to appear most prominently in marriage and parenting. Ironically, it shows up with those we love the most. Too often everyone *except* our spouses are the recipients of our best tone. There's something fundamentally wrong with this reality. When negative tone happens too often, your spouse will begin to lose respect for you, and emotional distance will become the norm.

A HEART ISSUE

What's behind the negative tone? Negativity unmasks the true feelings of the heart. Sometimes your heart issue may have little to do with your spouse and much more to do with how you're feeling about life in general and yourself in particular. Negativity is typically not about your spouse; it's more about what's brewing within your own heart.

Here's a question to ponder: Does your seemingly innocent choice of tone actually reveal a deeper, personal heart issue? If it does, then it's time to do everything you can to deal with what is lurking beneath the surface of your heart so you can excavate it and not allow it to negatively influence the way you communicate with and relate to your spouse. Far too many couples create negative habits early in the marriage, and those habits go unchecked and wind up accelerating the marital drift. Thankfully, the good news is that you can change your tone, your words, your intention of motive, and your heart so they're more positive. The power to choose the positive is in your control, just as our friend Nancy discovered.

She had been married to the love of her life for six years. Though she loved Greg, she knew their relationship was drifting into troubled waters. It wasn't just the tone of words they used with each other. Their tone was a reflection of the overall negative atmosphere they both had created in their home. Since being at home was such a negative experience, Greg found reasons to spend more time at work, on hobbies, with friends, and doing anything else to avoid that environment. As a result, Nancy began to fantasize about life without Greg. In fact, she found herself creating actual scenarios where she'd escape to find a better lover, husband, and friend. Even the idea of an affair—which had repulsed her in their first few years of marriage—was now bordering on desire as she entertained the opportunities she could create for herself.

Thankfully, a very loving and perceptive girlfriend from church asked Nancy out for coffee. The friend simply probed with an observation: "How's it going at home? It appears that you and Greg have a pretty strained relationship. He mentioned to my husband that the atmosphere at home and between you two is pretty negative."

Nancy felt the sting of that question, but instead of hiding in denial, she chose to open up and pour out her heart. She told this friend that she did indeed love her husband and confessed to drifting into some really poor communication and relationship habits. She admitted that she had developed a negative posture and promised her girlfriend that she would make immediate choices to be more positive and optimistic about Greg as a husband and about the future of their marriage.

That very night, Nancy made a commitment to becoming more optimistic. When Greg came home from work (late as usual), she chose to remain positive. She had fixed a nice meal, decorated the dinner table with the good plates, lit candles, and had his favorite music playing softly in the background. It was a striking difference to what they normally experienced at meals together. During dinner she thanked Greg for working so hard to provide for the comfort of their home and complimented him on things that were true about him that she hadn't expressed in months. She also held her tongue a few times when she would normally have said something negative. The result of this intentionally positive meal was a great evening that ended with a sexual intimacy they hadn't experienced in a long time.

Nancy felt great about her choice to go positive. She felt empowered. She realized that her commitment to have more positive communication and an optimistic outlook changed everything that night and gave her hope for the future. Greg hadn't necessarily acted any differently, but he definitely responded differently to the changes Nancy made in her tone. She knew she needed to make some significant adjustments and took intentional steps toward heart health and healing.

Within days she felt different and was pleasantly surprised to see Greg responding to her changes with more optimism of his own. As she chose to be positive, her words and tone changed because they were becoming a reflection of a renewed attitude. It was remarkable to see Greg become softer and kinder toward her as well. She didn't always respond perfectly, but when she'd take a step backward toward negativity, she would immediately recognize it, diagnose it as a heart issue, apologize to Greg for it, and head back in a positive direction.

Nancy told us that her marriage to Greg is strong and greatly improved because she didn't wait for him to change. She changed first. Today she can't even imagine being in the arms of someone else, when just months ago, she was dreaming about that escape. Nancy is the perfect illustration of a person who was courageous enough to make some heart-level changes that transformed her marriage from mediocre to remarkable.

It's doable—even for you. Now let's move away from all this negative talk and get you thinking about being more positive.

A POSITIVE MARRIAGE

John Gottman, one of the world's leading marriage researchers, whom we often quote, has found that the main difference between a stable and unstable marriage is the positive thoughts and actions spouses engage in toward each other.[1] If you want a healthy and satisfying marriage, you'll *both* need to share high levels of positivity. Fun, laughter, and optimism characterize marriages with a healthy emotional climate. Positivity isn't just about having fun as a couple or being at peace with yourself. It involves feeling emotionally healthy as individuals *and* as a couple.

As Dr. Neil Clark Warren observed, "No marriage can ever be stronger than the emotional health of the least healthy partner."[2] Once again, a healthy marriage requires self-evaluation, reflection on the condition of your heart, and a commitment to move in a positive direction. Remember, changing yourself is possible, though perhaps not easy; changing your spouse is impossible.

BEING POSITIVE ISN'T DENYING THE REALITY OF PAIN

The happiest, most fulfilled marriages we know of don't seem to have fewer problems than other marriages, but these couples do choose to be more positive. The quality of a marriage is more about perspective than circumstances. Your circumstances may not change, but your perspective, your attitude, and your outlook can all change *regardless of your situation.*

People who choose positive responses toward their spouses and their lives are simply happier. They have an underlying, predominant sense of well-being and a contentment that nourishes relationships. Research indicates that people who choose to be positive not only do better in their marriages; they're also healthier and more successful in their careers.[3] Positive people develop flexibility and a relational buoyancy that allow them to bounce back from challenges, setbacks, or negative circumstances.

My (Doug's) wife is one of the most easygoing humans I know. She's really flexible and positive. She doesn't go into denial when things are bad; she just chooses the more positive lane. In her words, "There's always a more positive route to take, and it's a lot more fun and beneficial for everyone around when I choose positivity. It definitely requires conscious and constant choices. Life isn't always easy, but I've come to understand that I make it more difficult on myself and others when I'm negative."

If you and/or your spouse aren't normally positive, you can choose to change. Once again, so much of a happy, healthy marriage comes down to choice.

YOU CAN LEARN TO BE MORE POSITIVE

Relational experts refer to this journey toward positivity as *learned optimism*. We love that phrase! When you learn to be optimistic, it changes your attitudes, outlook, and perspective—all of which results in a better tone and stronger communication in your marriage.

I (Jim) have a friend who has a challenging, high-maintenance marriage that's also a very good and strong one. I recently asked him, "How have you managed to have a successful relationship with all the issues you two have experienced?"

His answer was very enlightening:

> I've decided not to sweat the small stuff [but to] be optimistic toward my [very emotional] wife. I've conditioned my reflex reaction to be a positive one. Once I decided to meet her emotion [a.k.a. *drama*] with a positive response, it quickly changed me, and it has slowly changed her. When I responded in a negative way, it just fueled her emotional response. I saw that being positive worked in our marriage, and I continued making positive choices and practicing … until my reflex reaction was positive. I had opportunities to practice every day, and now it's just my natural response.

That's such a powerful story packed with solid advice. I knew he was doing something differently to make his marriage thrive. He made the courageous decisions to develop a new reaction, and over time it has paid off.

Here's the bottom line: your marriage needs to be filled with more positive than negative. It's that simple and that complex.

THE MAGIC RATIO

You need more convincing? Let's take a look at Gottman's research on how important it is to be positive in your marriage, as well as the idea of developing frequent, small positive acts toward your spouse. His "magic ratio" is five to one in terms of the balance of positive to negative interactions. Gottman found that marriages are significantly more likely to succeed when a couple's interactions are closer to the five-to-one ratio of positive versus negative (in other words, five positive interactions for every one negative interaction). According to Gottman, couples with more negative interactions than positive ones are typically headed for divorce.

So imagine for a moment that we've followed you and your spouse around with a video camera over the past several weeks. Every single conversation—including inflection (tone) and non-verbal communication (smiles, winks, smirks, eye rolls, gasps, looks of disgust, etc.)—has been recorded and transcribed into written form. The words and nonverbal actions are then sliced and diced into two clear-cut categories: positive and negative. Now we're going to post the results on the wall and closely evaluate your positive-to-negative ratio. How do you think you'd do? Would you be five-to-one positive or two-to-three negative or maybe even at one-to-one?

To help you move toward a five-to-one marriage, we recommend that you immediately begin to practice three specific actions.

1. KEEP ASKING THIS *ONE* VITAL QUESTION

One of the secrets of learning to become more positive in your marriage is to continually ask yourself a basic but core question: "Does this [issue, tension, etc.] really matter?"

Let's apply this important question to the toothpaste tube that you presumably both share. Perhaps your spouse grew up squeezing the middle of the tube, and you roll it neatly from the bottom (like Jesus probably did). It bugs you that your spouse doesn't do it "right," right?

Now to our one vital question: Does it *really* matter? Yes, we know you *wish* your spouse would do it the way you do. We even understand that it matters to you. We're also aware that it makes you mad and triggers negative thoughts. We get it. Now drop the emotion for a second and ask yourself, "Does this toothpaste-tube tension *really* matter?" Of course not! Do you have a preference? Absolutely! And your preference is right to you, but it doesn't *really* matter in the broader scope of your marriage. Since you may be getting a little emotional about your toothpaste quandary, let's pause for a second. Take a deep breath. One more. Exhale. Feel better? Now let's continue.

We know that illustration may have been tough on you. Actually, we hope you're laughing with us (at least a little) and have grasped the principle behind this vital question. If so, let's slice this question another way: "How important is this issue to your marriage?" Does this issue make the top-ten list of things you want to continue to battle over?

Here's the truth you must embrace during your first few years of marriage: *you simply can't have strong opinions and care deeply about everything*. That will destroy your marriage. There are only so many things that a happy, healthy, and vibrant person can ultimately care about 1,440 minutes every day. There's just not enough time to care deeply about every single frustration. When little things are making you angry, you won't have any room to be positive. You can't make everything a big deal in your marriage. This truth requires you to relax on a few things and figure out how to let them go so they don't continue to fuel negativity. If you embrace this basic truth and ask the question often, they can guide you toward some very important course corrections.

Let's face it, you didn't marry a perfect person (and we hate to pop your bubble, but your spouse didn't marry one either!). Some things will bug you, and you'll have to ask yourself, "Does this *really* matter?" We strongly believe that some things *should* really matter—addictions, abuse, neglect, and unkindness, for example—but so much happens in marriage that some things just shouldn't matter, or you'll be angry all the time and negativity will flow from your heart into your thoughts, your tone, and ultimately your actions. Yuck! No one wants that, and no one wants to live with someone who is negative and angry all the time. If you keep asking, "Does this *really* matter?" you'll find yourself engaging in fewer battles with your spouse and enjoying more peace in your marriage.

2. PRACTICE GRATITUDE

Doug often teases me (Jim) and says that I have a way of weaving a certain theme into just about every message I give. It's what I call "thank therapy." It's my life message, so I confess that I'm a bit fanatical about it. But I'm okay being teased about it as long as you grasp this life-changing idea. The practice of gratitude has become the key to who I am as a person and has definitely been the foundation of my forty-plus-year marriage to Cathy.

Thank therapy is simply focusing on what you can be thankful for rather than what you could complain about. I challenge people to develop the *daily* habit of writing down twenty reasons why they're thankful. I know it sounds like a lot, but coming up with twenty reasons is the secret sauce that forces you into a more positive mindset. This discipline isn't a magic wand to eliminate your negative circumstances, but it is magical in how quickly it works to change your attitude. It's nearly impossible to feel both grateful and negative at the same time. Thank therapy works for me, it works for Doug (even though he teases me), and it will work for you and your marriage. Thankfulness wins over negativity.

A few years ago, Cathy and I took a most romantic trip up the coast of California to the beautiful beach town of Carmel. Our time together was simply enchanting. It was filled with long walks along the breathtaking coast, intimate conversations over lingering meals, and the freedom of extended times of romance. Really, it was all so stunning!

As we prepared to drive back home along the Pacific Coast Highway, we reflected on how wonderful our time had been and how it had refueled our relationship. Driving down the winding road along the cliffs, we saw dolphins playing in the ocean and majestic birds highlighting the beauty of God's creation. Then out of nowhere, Cathy looked at me and said matter-of-factly, "Jim, I think you're getting a double chin!"

Immediately the dolphins disappeared, the majestic birds flew away, and all that scenic beauty transformed into an emotion called *hurt*. It's one thing for Doug to tease me about my obsession with thank therapy, but it was just plain mean for my wife to bring up a body flaw and pop my fantasy bubble.

I'm not sure what Cathy was expecting me to say in response, but believe me, I was not only hurt; I was angry. My default response to being hurt is to go quiet, and I got very quiet—double-chin quiet. I didn't speak for forty-five minutes as we continued driving. Cathy seemed so engrossed in the beautiful scenery that I'm not even sure she noticed my silent, passive-aggressive behavior. As she was whistling, I was stewing ... until I heard the "still, small voice" in my head say that I needed to practice gratefulness. It was time for thank therapy.

So with gritted teeth and a double chin, I silently prayed, *Thank You for Cathy, even if she thinks I'm getting fat.* I then added, *And thank You for the incredible time we had. Thank You for the wonderful mother Cathy is to our girls. Thank You for giving her to me as the most amazing partner in our ministry to families ...* And the list grew. After naming about twenty reasons I was grateful for Cathy, I leaned toward her, gave her a kiss, and said, "I love you, Cathy!"

She looked at me with a smirk and said, "Oh, I thought you were mad at me because I mentioned you're getting a double chin."

For the moment at least, the practice of thankfulness worked for me, and it will work for you too.

3. WEAR POSITIVE GOGGLES

At a recent marriage conference, I (Doug) passed out a pair of cheap swim goggles to each couple in the audience. First, I had all the men put on the goggles and then look at their wives. It was pretty funny watching grown men maneuvering the goggles in an attempt to look cool. Then it was the women's turn to try them on. Many were conscious of their hair, and it was obvious they weren't pleased they were doing such a silly activity.

After all the couples had tried on the goggles, I said, "Part of the struggle of wearing these goggles is, one, they're uncomfortable and don't feel natural; two, they need adjustments to make them fit; and three, they require practicing in water before they'll work the way they're designed to."

I then asked the couples to place the goggles in a conspicuous spot in their bedrooms or bathrooms (e.g., on a dresser, in the shower, on the bathroom sink, etc.) as a daily reminder to see their spouses in a more positive light.

If you don't want to drift in your marriage, you have to put on your positive goggles every day. As I told the couples at the marriage conference: this may feel uncomfortable and unnatural at first; you'll probably need to make some adjustments, and you'll most likely have to practice before positivity becomes a default response. But once you make the bold and courageous decision to move from negativity to a more positive tone in your marriage, we're confident you'll begin to see your marriage change for the better. Being positive about each other isn't a feeling; it's a daily choice you have the power to make. So go ahead. Put on your positive goggles!

QUESTIONS

1. How would you rate your interactions as a couple using the positive-to-negative ratio?
2. How has negativity affected your relationship?
3. List twenty reasons why you're thankful for your spouse, and then take the time to share those reasons with him or her.

Chapter Seven

•

FIGHT FEAR

One June, Cathy casually asked me (Doug), "Do you want to go to Kyle and Lydia's wedding over Labor Day weekend? It's in Fresno."

Here's what immediately raced through my mind: *I really like Kyle and Lydia. They're great. But the thought of driving to Fresno (about 250 miles away) in Southern California traffic on a holiday weekend is about as appealing as having my teeth pulled while being held hostage at a McDonald's PlayPlace filled with five year olds hopped up on candy. I'm not sure I'd want to go to my own kids' weddings if they chose that date and location.*

Wisely, I didn't tell her my thoughts. Instead, I kindly responded, "No, not really. That's essentially the last weekend of our summer. I'd rather be at home."

She apparently had those same thoughts and said, "You're right, that's the last official weekend of our summer. I'll RSVP a no."

Super! One more calendar decision checked off our list.

About a month later, Cathy was looking over a pile of mail and asked me, "What did we decide on Kyle and Lydia's wedding? Do you want to go? I'd kinda like to go, but I could be talked out of it."

I jumped quickly on that opening. "Babe, we already decided we weren't going because it's Labor Day weekend. Remember?"

Cathy replied, "That's right. I forgot to RSVP. Summer has been so busy. I wish that wedding wasn't in Fresno."

Crisis averted—or so I thought.

Fast-forward to about nine weeks after our original conversation and about three weeks before the wedding. We were sitting at El Pollo Loco (the Crazy Chicken), a local fast-food diner, where we were catching up and talking about our fall calendar.

Cathy said, "I know you've said no to Kyle and Lydia's wedding, but I would really like to go. [Wait for it; here it comes] I feel like I say yes to a lot of your requests, and I wish you would say yes to more of mine."

Boom! Hello, conflict. I guess we were going to do this in a crowded restaurant named after an insane chicken. Personally, I hate these types of tensions and the ensuing arguments. They're just not fun. For thirty minutes or so, there was attacking, defensiveness, and frustration. Neither of us was budging on our opinions—the ingredients of a marriage fight. There was no yelling—that's not our style—but there were definitely hurt feelings.

Later, as we were driving home, I thought, *Great timing!* (Read: sarcasm.) *Of course we'd have a fight on the day I'm working on the conflict chapter for my marriage book.*

In that little booth, surrounded by a bunch of strangers, Cathy and I had conflict. It wasn't our first argument, and it won't be our last. Whether you've been married more than thirty years like we have or you're in your first few years of marriage, conflict will happen.

Yes, *every* marriage. Love. Conflict. Unmet expectations. Hurt. Forgiveness. Reconciliation. Apologies. Feelings. Mess. All of those apply to every single marriage—yours too. Because of that, we believe this is a very important chapter, and the principles we're going to teach you can help in big ways. Your marriage journey will definitely include some storms, and at times your relationship will feel as if it's quickly drifting off course, but we want to offer some guidance to help you avoid a marital shipwreck. *Conflict is inevitable, but misery is optional.*

FIGHTS HAPPEN IN GOOD MARRIAGES TOO

A big-picture relational truth that can serve as a foundation for understanding marital conflict is this: *relationships are messy.* You married an imperfect person, and your spouse happened to marry one too. As a result of human imperfection, people hurt each other.

Author Denis de Rougemont once said, "Why should neurotic, selfish, immature people suddenly become angels when they fall in love."[1] That statement not only makes us laugh; it's also so true. When two imperfect people merge their lives into one, things are bound to get a little messy. Newly married couples are often under the impression that saying "I do" on their wedding days will fix the issues that sparked premarital feuds. Unfortunately, the cost of a wedding won't buy you freedom from conflict. Issues that appeared *before* marriage will inevitably be there *after* marriage, and some of those same issues would continue to be present if you got divorced and married someone else. Marriage doesn't stop conflict; it actually becomes a source of additional conflict.

Conflict happens; that's not the issue. The issue is how you respond to it.

Marriage researchers have discovered that happy couples have just as many differences of opinion and conflicts as unhappy couples who divorce. The compelling difference is that happy couples have learned to deal with conflict in more constructive, mature, healthy, and positive ways. How a couple communicates and handles conflict is the trait most closely linked to the success or failure of their marriage.[2]

The good news is that communication and conflict-resolution skills aren't genetic traits you're born with; they're *learned* traits. If you learn how to fight fair and forgive often, there is great hope for your future. To get us started, let's consider where all this tension in our marriages comes from.

THE FEAR LURKING BEHIND MARITAL CONFLICT

Because you're not a perfect human being, you'll say and do things that wound, frustrate, hurt, and damage your spouse. And since you didn't marry Jesus (who is perfect) or a robot (that's predictable and unemotional), your spouse will say and do things that hurt you. Certain words, looks, and actions will poke at very real feelings, and it's game on—fight time. Most spouses know how to push each other's buttons.

Here's what happens when your spouse hurts your feelings: *your fear is awakened.* To simplify this complex idea, try thinking of it this way: Normally your fear is taking a nap on the couch. When your spouse pushes your hot button (think of it as pushing a doorbell), the ringing noise awakens your fear, which jumps up to respond to the threat (the one that pushed your hot button). That's the origin of conflict: fear is awakened. The kind of fear we're referring to isn't associated with being scared because you walk into a dark room and see a spider or because you encounter a creepy clown. We're talking about *relational fear,* such as the fear of

> rejection;
> disconnection;
> control or manipulation;
> failure;
> invalidation;
> worthlessness;
> unhappiness; and
> loss.

Let me (Doug) show you how this works by returning to the conflict Cathy and I had about the wedding in Fresno. My primary relational fear is not being good enough. That's my main hot button, and I don't like it when that fear is awakened. In the El Pollo Loco scenario, these words from Cathy pushed my button: "I feel like I say yes to a lot of your requests, and I wish you would say yes to more of mine." Ding dong! Hot button pushed. My fear of not being a good enough husband was now awakened, alerted, and ready to answer the door for a fight.

I could write an entire chapter sharing stories of how that fear began when I was a child, but here's the short version: I grew up in a shame-based parenting environment. It wasn't evil or rotten or bad. Even though my parents loved me, I felt as if I was never good enough. If I got an A on a report card, my mom might have said, "I wonder if you would have gotten an A-plus if you'd given it a little more effort or done some extra credit."

What I heard was, "You're not a good enough student."

If I played in a baseball game and went 3–4 with two doubles, I might have heard, "Great game, Doug. Just think, if you'd been a little faster, you could have beat out that ground ball and been four for four. Wouldn't that have been amazing?"

Here's the truth: going 3–4 *is* amazing, but it was short of perfection.

To this day I believe with all my heart that my parents were doing the best they could. They didn't know they were planting and watering seeds of fear that would grow stronger and make me more vulnerable to its harmful effects. They most likely believed I was good enough, but I didn't hear it that way. I embraced a lie instead. And that lie gave birth to fear. *What if it's true? What if I'm really not good enough?*

The lie that I'm not good enough was written on my heart at a young age. I believed it for so long that it became part of my relationship script. Today this lie shows up in my marriage, my parenting, my work, and my friendships. Most of the time, my fear is sleeping. The healthier I become, the deeper this fear sleeps and the more difficult it is to wake it.

I know I'm not alone. Everyone has relational fears to some degree. You might be so emotionally healthy that it takes a lot before your fear is awakened. That's great! But the opposite may also be true; your fear(s) may be easily triggered.

In this chapter, we'll help you identify your primary fear (hot button), but first let's look at how your fear can lead to negative responses that push, poke, awaken, and agitate your spouse's primary fear and trigger a negative conflict cycle.

When fear is awakened, negative responses quickly follow. Fear doesn't wake up happy. It wakes up armed and ready to respond in a negative way. It then races to the door of conflict, ready to either fight or flee. Responses can vary at the door: One person might *explode*, screaming and expressing anger over fear being awakened ("Let's fight"). Another person might open the door of conflict, quickly shut it (flee), and *implode* (the opposite of exploding). Imploding is when a person stuffs anger to avoid talking about it. Both ways of dealing with fear being awakened and agitated—either exploding or imploding—lead to negative responses.

Negative responses create additional conflict and disconnection. When you either fling open the door to fight or slam the door and flee, your spouse feels your negative response. Here's where it can get really messy: your initial negative response actually pushes your spouse's hot button, awakening his or her fear. Once your spouse's fear is awakened, he or she will respond negatively to you. Guess what happens next? Your spouse's negative response triggers your fear again, and you do the same thing you did last time: respond negatively. This starts a cycle: You feel hurt and react. Your reaction hurts your spouse, who responds negatively. You're hurt again and respond negatively. And round and round it goes.

Look at the following graphic and consider my conflict with Cathy over the wedding. When she expressed her disappointment in me (Doug) for not wanting to go to the wedding, she pushed my hot button, and my fear of not being a good enough husband awakened. My default negative response was to withdraw emotionally (implode). When I responded this way, it pushed Cathy's hot button, which is the fear of being disconnected. When her button was pushed, her negative response was to shut down emotionally. Her response poked again at my fear of not being a good enough husband, and my negative response (imploding) set in motion the second round of the cycle.

This graphic, sometimes referred to as "the Fear Chase,"[3] illustrates how our fears (hot buttons) and responses end up chasing each other.[4]

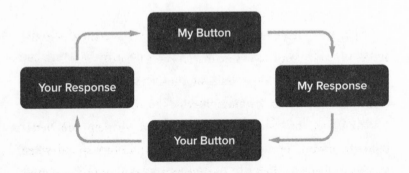

What Cathy and I originally thought was the issue (the wedding) wasn't ultimately the real issue. The main issue was fear. Most of the time, what couples describe as their issues aren't actually their real issues. They could argue about sex, money, time, in-laws, weddings, whatever, but the real issue is that their fear was awakened.

THE FEAR CHASE

Putting these principles into practice in your marriage has the potential to change the way you argue with your spouse and make the outcomes of conflict more beneficial for the health of your marriage. Your spouse isn't the enemy in your marriage; you'll learn to fight the fear instead of fighting each other. You have two enemies: the first is your unique primary fear, and the second is the negative way you respond when that fear is awakened. If we can get both of you to see these as your real enemies, you'll learn to resolve conflict more thoughtfully, love each other more deeply, and move toward forgiveness and healing more quickly.

Now it's time to make this El Pollo Loco illustration personal and practical for you. To ensure that the Fear Chase principles make sense to you, we're going to lead you through a little exercise. You'll need to have a notebook or journal handy to write in.

Think of this exercise as an experiment to help you better understand your fears and the way you typically respond when they're awakened. After you discover your primary fear and your normal negative response, we'll see how it chases your spouse's unique fear.

Ready? Let's try this!

As you begin this exercise, we encourage you to embrace an adventurous spirit. Be ready to experiment with this concept of fighting your fear instead of fighting each other, and let's see if it yields any new discoveries for your marriage.

START WITH A RECENT CONFLICT

Think of a recent conflict or argument you had with your spouse. If you're reading this with your spouse, it's not necessary that you both recall the same fight. One of you could think of last night's conflict, and the other could think of an argument you had last month.

When you have a conflict in mind, write the details in your journal. What was the argument about?

Next, answer these questions:

> What bothered you about this conflict?
> Why did you feel anger, hurt, or frustration?

Don't try to answer the questions for your spouse. Answer for yourself. In a few minutes, you'll compare your responses and talk about them, but for now, we want you to talk about your *own* fear and negative response.

Did you think of a recent conflict and answer the questions? If so, move on to the next step. If not, finish this step before you continue.

IDENTIFY YOUR PRIMARY FEAR

One of the easiest ways to identify your primary fear (your hot button) is to think about the conflict you identified in the previous section and ask yourself, "Why did that particular conflict bother me so much?" The more you dig for the real answer to this question, the closer you'll get to discovering your primary fear.

This is the most difficult and important step in the process because it requires you to think deeply about why you feel hurt during fights with your spouse. Don't give up and settle for a superficial answer like "It just made me mad," or "I don't know. I guess I'm easily triggered." What's the *real* reason it made you mad? What might you have been afraid of?

Take some time to really think about it. We promise it will be worth the effort if you dig a little deeper to discover your primary fear. When you finally pinpoint it, you'll be on your way to healthier marital conflict resolution.

Here's an example of what we mean by digging deeper:

> **Counselor:** What is the most recent conflict you two have had?
>
> **Husband:** Oh, that's an easy one. We just got in a huge fight over how much time I work.
>
> **Counselor (to the wife):** What bothers you about your husband's work hours?
>
> **Wife:** I don't like how much he works. He spends more time at work than he does at home.

Counselor: Okay, but what bothers you about your husband spending more time at work than at home?

Wife: The kids really miss him a lot.

Counselor: What bothers you about the kids missing him so much?

Wife: It feels like they're not important enough for him to spend time with … and I'm not either.

Counselor: Okay, it sounds like what you're saying is that when your husband spends more time at work than at home, that makes you feel *unwanted* or *unimportant*. Is that right?

Wife: Yes, that is exactly what I feel.[5]

After a little bit of digging, the wife in this example discovered that her primary fear is being unwanted or considered unimportant. Notice that she didn't arrive at her primary fear right away. She had to be prompted to get to the real reason.

Now at this point, the counselor would do the same thing with the husband and ask him, "What bothers you about your wife complaining about your work hours?" And they'd keep digging until he uncovered his primary fear.

To make it a little easier to discover your primary fear, we've included a list of the top twenty relational fears. Look them over and identify the ones you typically feel during a conflict with your spouse. Then write down the primary fear that applies to your most recent conflict.

TOP TWENTY RELATIONAL FEARS[6]

Being rejected	Being judged
Feeling disconnected	Feeling lonely
Feeling like a failure	Feeling powerless
Being misunderstood	Being invalidated
Feeling defective	Feeling inferior
Feeling worthless	Being devalued
Feeling humiliated	Being abandoned
Being unimportant	Being ignored
Being unwanted	Being disliked
Feeling I can't trust others	Feeling unhappy

If you're struggling to identify your primary fear, don't get hung up on it. You can always go back through this list again and think more deeply about the words that best describe it. When you've identified your primary fear, write it in your journal. If you're still not sure, write down what you think it might be.

Good job! Now let's move on.

DESCRIBE YOUR TYPICAL RESPONSE WHEN YOUR FEAR IS AWAKENED

When your spouse pushes your hot button and your fear is awakened, you'll typically respond a certain way. The following list includes some of the most common negative responses. Identify your typical reactions and list them in your journal. Then circle the one that seems to be your default response.

COMMON NEGATIVE RESPONSES[7]

Withdrawing	Escalating
Shifting into earn-it mode	Clinging to negative beliefs
Blaming	Exaggerating
Having tantrums	Going into denial
Invalidating	Becoming defensive
Clinging	Being passive-aggressive
Caretaking	Acting out
Going into fix-it mode	Complaining/criticizing
Striking out	Manipulating
Becoming angry or enraged	Catastrophizing
Shutting down emotionally	Expressing humor
Displaying sarcasm	Minimizing
Rationalizing	Becoming indifferent
Abdicating	Abandoning yourself

You can return to this list at a later time if you're having trouble identifying your default response.

Congratulations! You've listed some terms that describe your primary fear and your typical negative response when your fear is triggered.

When you have the opportunity to talk about the Fear Chase cycle with your spouse, share with each other your primary fear and negative response. We encourage you not to rehash past fights. All you need to say is, "I think my primary fear is _____, and when my fear is triggered, my negative response is usually _____." It's important that you listen carefully and respond to each other in a tender way. Listening is a great way to communicate love. Be extrasensitive here. No one loves talking about his or her fears. Just own your part.

After you've shared your fears and responses with each other, it might be helpful to copy the Fear Chase diagram from page 124 into your journal and write your and your spouse's primary fears and responses in the appropriate spaces. This can help you visualize how your primary fears and responses chase each other. Once you understand this negative Fear Chase cycle, discuss how you can change it by being more sensitive to each other's primary fears. For example, I (Doug) know that Cathy is afraid of disconnection, so I don't want to trigger that fear in the way I communicate with her.

CHOOSE A MORE POSITIVE RESPONSE

The next time your fear is awakened, how would you like to respond in a more positive manner? What would be the most honoring way for you to engage with your spouse? Identify a response from the following list that best reflects the type of person you want to become; then record it in your journal.

Accepting	Compassionate	Nurturing
Nondefensive	Energetic	Supportive
Vulnerable	Hopeful	Encouraging
Caring	Respectful	Giving
Engaging	Open	Welcoming
Peaceful	Intimate	Kind
Present	Gentle	Settled
Responsible	Good listener	Trustworthy
Empathetic	Merciful	Honest
Humble	Loving	Reliable

Inclusive	Patient	Positive
Self-controlled	Forgiving	Joyful
Transparent	Other:	

Take a moment to share with each other your ideal positive responses. As one of you shares, the other should listen and affirm, not make derogatory comments. (In other words, no fair saying, "Yeah, right. I can't see you *ever* responding like that!")

We're well aware that this is a lot to digest, and you may need to revisit this chapter a few times for it to stick. But before we move on to the very important topic of forgiveness, we want to make one more comment about the Fear Chase. It's essential that you realize you are *100 percent responsible* for your hot button and response and *0 percent responsible* for your spouse's hot button and response. You know by now that you can't change your spouse, but you can change yourself. You have control over your hot buttons and reactions. This is an important point and a reminder that you have the power of choice. You can choose a better response. You can choose to get help with that lie written on your heart. You can speak truth to each other and help bring out the best in one another. You're no longer a victim of your past circumstances. You can choose a new, positive way to resolve conflict.

THE ULTIMATE GOAL: FORGIVENESS

When someone is seriously injured, one of the primary first-aid instructions is to control or stop the bleeding. In marriage, an effective way to control or stop the emotional bleeding that flows during the Fear Chase is to forgive. Forgiveness is an amazing course correction that will be required hundreds of times on your marital journey. If you (or your spouse) struggle with forgiveness, you're choosing to allow the bleeding to continue in the confines of a self-imposed prison. Unforgiving people put themselves in a prison of anger, resentment, and hurt.

Cathy and I (Jim) have created a simple forgiveness phrase that has become part of our relationship script: "Dig no holes" (or at least no deep holes). This relational metaphor is a reminder that we don't want to damage our marriage foundation by causing unnecessary conflict. (You've probably heard the expression "You're digging yourself into a deeper hole.") If you've been digging holes and damaging the foundation of your marriage, you need to repair and refill those holes quickly with confession, repentance, and forgiveness. Forgiveness is the key to dealing with conflict, as well as the ultimate goal. It's the only pathway to relational happiness and finding peace, contentment, and satisfaction in your marriage.

People often say, "Time heals all wounds." Our experience is that this isn't true. Time doesn't heal *all* wounds; for that type of healing, we need forgiveness. The great writer William Faulkner once wrote, "The past is never dead. It's not even past."[8] Although he wasn't writing about marriage, it definitely applies to marriage. In your marriage, when there's pain, tension, conflict, fighting, anger, or any other wound, it's *very present*. It lives in the here and now. This makes it difficult to forgive. Our amazing, God-given memories keep pain fresh. If you're struggling to move beyond a specific hurt, there are really only four options for dealing with it and only one that will ultimately heal the pain.

1. You can try to forget the offense. This would be great if it was actually possible, but good luck with this inept strategy. Trying to forget a problem with your spouse isn't a viable option. Some people think the pain can be resolved if they leave the marriage and move on, even running away and creating physical distance from it, such as moving to a different place and starting over. The pain and memory then recede into the background or get buried, so they seem resolved. But humans are seldom able to truly forget the pain other humans inflict on them.

2. You can repress the offense. Repressing an offense (or imploding) just delays the inevitable. The dysfunction related to the pain will leak out and be revealed in your thoughts and actions. Unfortunately, repression never works in the long term and doesn't allow the necessary relational healing to take place.

3. You can hold on to the offense. This is perhaps the strategy couples employ most often. One woman told us she'd been married for thirty-eight years and is still mad at her husband for forgetting their first anniversary. Sounds crazy, right? It's true! Yes, he should have remembered their anniversary, but that was thirty-seven years ago, and she still occasionally brings out that offense and uses it to manipulate and shame her husband. After talking with her, we learned she was holding on to a lot of other hurt as well. We were actually surprised they're still married, although we weren't surprised it's a terrible marriage that is dangerously off course. Holding on to the pain of the past and using it to beat up your spouse simply keeps the pain alive.

4. You can forgive the offense. This is the lone option that truly works. Forgiveness is the only action you can take to release the negative events of your past. Forgiveness is the choice that leads to healing for both the giver and the receiver. You may need to forgive the same offense 500 times before you really feel like you've forgiven your spouse. The idea of repetitive forgiveness originated with Jesus, who raised the stakes when He said we're to forgive seventy times seven, if needed.[9] We don't think the magic number is 490 times, but the deeper and heart-freeing principle is to keep forgiving until your prison door unlocks and you're free of isolation, entrapment, resentment, and the chains of holding a grudge. The goal of forgiveness is freedom.

During the first few years of marriage, couples develop patterns (or habits) of relating to each other. We believe it's very important to create a pattern of forgiveness in your marriage as well. Make forgiveness and sincere apologies part of your relational language. If you know that the end result of a conflict will be healing and forgiveness, you can endure conflict. You can address the fears that are fueling your negative responses and work together toward healing. Forgiveness is the destination you're aiming for in your marriage journey.

Justin and Jenna had been married for three years when they talked with us at one of our marriage conferences. To say that Jenna was mad at her husband is an understatement. She was fuming and boiling over with anger. In fact, we thought she was mad at us too, because we had said that deep connection in marriage can happen only with forgiveness. With an intense stare and an angry tone, she told us, "Justin is a liar, and I just don't know if I can ever trust him again. On top of that, you guys are saying that I'm supposed to forgive him, and everything will be okay."

While that wasn't exactly what we had said, we knew we weren't going to be able to clarify anything until we heard what Justin did to her. Jenna explained, "Last week, Justin told me he had to work late. I thought I was being patient and generous to tell him that would be fine, even though there are times when I feel like he loves his job more than he loves me."

We asked, "So what happened?"

She snapped, "Justin didn't work late. He and two of his friends went to dinner and to a college basketball game. Furthermore, he didn't admit to me what he had done. I saw a post on one of his friends' Facebook accounts, with Justin and the guys holding beers up at the game." She then repeated her earlier threat: "I don't know if I can ever trust him again."

We looked at Justin. He shrugged his shoulders and said, "I really screwed up. I wanted to go to the game with my friends, but she hates it if I do anything social without her. So I lied. When she confronted me, I confessed to what I had done. I sincerely apologized. There's no question; I was an idiot. Regardless, she didn't seem to want to hear it and said some horrible things, so I got defensive and fought back." Smirking, he concluded, "It wasn't our best interaction."

He then looked at his wife and said, "Honey, I really am sorry. I admit that I was totally in the wrong when I lied. Again, I ask you to forgive me."

It appeared as if Jenna either didn't hear those words or ignored Justin's apology, because she went right on telling us what a jerk he was for lying. It was messy.

Here's our slant: Justin was 100 percent wrong to lie to his wife. Behavior like this will eventually erode the relationship and had already eroded Jenna's trust.

We asked Jenna if this was something Justin did all the time, and she responded, "No, not really. But I don't think I can trust him ever again."

We knew we weren't going to resolve this issue during the fifteen-minute stretch break at the conference. They had multiple communication and trust issues that were already deeply rooted in their new marriage. We suggested that they talk through this problem with a counselor or a pastor who could spend time getting to the core of their issues (fear).

As they walked back to their seats, we looked at each other and said, "He was wrong, but she'll need to find a way to forgive him, or that relationship is doomed."

Jenna may need to learn that forgiving and forgetting are two different actions. Ultimately, by holding back forgiveness, Jenna is punishing herself more than hurting Justin. The more she learns to genuinely forgive him, the easier it will be for her to forget his infraction. But even if she never forgets the offense, she needs to stop bringing up the same issue, which conveniently ignites her anger.

Like so many other important marriage principles, forgiveness is a choice—a divinely motivated one at that. It doesn't just happen. It's an action you must consciously practice if you want to win in your marriage. It has to become part of your script of relating to each other. It's essential to understand that forgiving your spouse isn't dependent on him or her being worthy of forgiveness. Forgiveness has very little to do with justice.

Jesus illustrated this type of forgiveness during His interaction with a woman caught in the act of adultery.[10] The townspeople brought her to Jesus and referenced the Old Testament law that clearly said she should be stoned for her sin (justice). Jesus looked at the guilty woman with eyes of compassion and then spoke to the gathered crowd: "Let any one of you who is without sin be the first to throw a stone at her."

After hearing those words, people slowly walked away, admitting their own sinfulness and tossing their rocks of judgment aside.

Jesus then looked at the humiliated woman and asked, "Where are [your accusers]? Has no one condemned you?"

Realizing they had all left the scene, she replied, "No one, sir."

Then in one of the greatest examples of forgiveness, Jesus said, "Then neither do I condemn you.... Go now and leave your life of sin."

Jesus recognized the woman had sinned, but He mercifully offered her forgiveness. She didn't deserve it or earn it, but she received the forgiveness He extended to her, as well as His loving challenge to go and live differently.

You have the ability to fight fear, forgive each other, and live differently. You have the power to choose to be either a spouse who allows conflict to make you bitter or a spouse who becomes better because you choose to forgive. Our hope and prayer is that you will choose the freedom and healing of forgiveness.

QUESTIONS

1. Can you think of anything from your past, including your childhood, that might have contributed to your fear buttons?

2. If you could go back in time, what would you say to your spouse when he or she was wounded and that particular lie was written on his or her heart? (For example, if your spouse's dad told your spouse in second grade that he or she was worthless, what would you have said to that eight year old?)

3. What are some rules for dealing with conflict in your relationship that you both can agree on for the future health of your marriage?

Chapter Eight

•

HAVE GREAT SEX

Did you know you could be on drugs legally and not even know it? Seriously. Researchers have found that during physical intimacy, couples have elevated levels of the hormone oxytocin.[1] This hormone is referred to as the "romance cocktail" because it influences sexual desire. But for many couples—even newlywed types—as the years progress, they find themselves yearning for a deeper physical connection and wondering what happened to their sex lives.

If you aren't experiencing romance and sexual intimacy on a regular basis, you could be drifting toward disconnection and emotional pain. When couples drift sexually, the marriage relationship becomes strained to the point of brokenness, anger looms just beneath the surface, and spouses have strong, hurtful feelings toward each other that are directly connected to a lack of physical fulfillment. Feelings like rejection, hurt, alienation, resentment, and an overall sense of being unloved slowly surface. When this happens, the worst is often assumed:

- "She doesn't really love me."
- "He's not attracted to me anymore."
- "She only cares about the kids."
- "He is probably having an affair."

How can something intended to be such an incredible experience drift into *average* so quickly and create friction in a marriage? The sexual drift happens for a number of possible reasons:

- Passion fades and routine appears.
- Busyness replaces romance.
- Couples bring sexual issues and hang-ups with them into the marriage, and those issues don't get resolved.
- One or both partners use pornography, which induces a false, diverted sense of intimacy.
- Frustration escalates over the frequency of sex, and apathy and anger soon follow.

We wish we could point to just *one* primary reason, but we hear all kinds of comments from couples:

- "When we have sex, it's good, but we just don't make it a priority."
- "She's a good person, but we both work hard, and by the time we crawl into bed, we're miles apart relationally and sexually even though we're only six inches apart physically."

- "He doesn't appear interested in sex anymore, and nothing I do seems to ignite his desires."
- "She never wants to have sex, and there's no good explanation other than 'I'm not interested.' The rejection is intense and painful."

While there's no single reason or solution for the sexual drift, we've learned from counseling hundreds of couples that if you don't deal with your sexual struggles in the early years of your marriage, you'll continue to struggle twenty, thirty, and even forty years later. These types of issues don't simply disappear. We've also learned something fascinating: a lot of couples don't like talking about their sex lives. It's understandable that they might not want to talk to us about their sexual struggles, but they don't like talking to *each other* about them either.

SEX AS A THERMOMETER

The opposite of all this negativity is also true: great sex can scream "great marriage." The key to building a healthy, vibrant marriage is laying a strong sexual foundation from the beginning. Psychologist and marriage expert Kevin Leman summarized it well: "Having a great sex life is an exhilarating experience; it can bond a husband and wife in a way that's unequaled in human experience."[2] To put it in simple terms, "Happy sex life, happy couple."

During the first few years of marriage, couples who learn to clarify their expectations and communicate openly about sex are better able to make the transition from the newness of their sexual relationship to more intimate, enduring passion. Couples can often measure how content and fulfilled they feel in their marriage based on the quality of sex and satisfaction in the sex life.

Researchers have found that "individuals in happy marriages are much more satisfied with the amount of affection they receive from their partner than unhappily married couples.... The sexual relationship acts as an emotional thermometer in that it reflects a couple's satisfaction with other aspects of their relationship. In other words, a good sexual relationship is often the outcome of a good emotional relationship between partners."[3]

I (Doug) concur with these findings and can confidently state that I've never counseled a couple who was having major problems in their marriage and a mutually satisfying sex life at the same time. I strongly believe that the physical connection in a marriage mirrors the emotional connection.

GET A CLEAR PICTURE OF A HEALTHY SEX LIFE

Many couples can't form a healthy picture of sexuality because of all the unhealthy images and messages rolling around in their minds. Some have to work really hard to turn off or tone down the dysfunctional messages they received prior to marriage. In his excellent book *The Mingling of Souls*, Matt Chandler wrote, "Clearly, we are a culture simultaneously obsessed with relationships and sex, but dysfunctional in our approaches to them."[4] Sadly, part of this dysfunction comes from the poor teaching many of us received earlier in life that seemingly communicated sex was *bad*. Or if that wasn't the overt message, the subtle message we heard while being taught to wait for sex until marriage was *"Sex is bad, so save it for the one you really love."* That's such a twisted message and couldn't be further from the truth.

Famed author Fredrick Buechner wrote, "Contrary to [what some believe], sex is not sin. Contrary to Hugh Hefner [founder of *Playboy*], it's not salvation either. Like nitroglycerin, [sex] can be used either to blow up bridges or heal hearts."[5] In the context of a healthy marriage, sex can be a beautiful, positive expression of your love for each other.

Thankfully, God isn't sexually repressed, and one way to get a healthy perspective on sex is to understand the beautiful, God-given design for sexuality. If lies about sex were somehow imprinted on your heart, or you adopted negative messages before you married, please hear that the expression of sex between you and your spouse is neither crude nor inappropriate nor something that should induce guilt. The truth is that your sexuality and its expression are gifts from God that need to be nurtured and used and enjoyed in your marriage so that sex doesn't become routine, stale, or problematic. Sex is an important part of God's overall plan for marital enjoyment and connection.

God designed sex within marriage not only to be good but also to *feel* good. Sex is intended for pleasure. A few years ago at a marriage conference, I (Doug) was speaking about the beauty of God's design for sex, and three simple words I said triggered a gasp from my Christian audience: "Consider the clitoris." I didn't intend for my words to be shocking. I wanted to emphasize the thoughtfulness of God's design. As you probably know, a woman's clitoris doesn't serve any biological function other than physical pleasure. That's pretty amazing handiwork, and it confirms that God isn't against sexual pleasure. Sex was His idea, and sexual pleasure and orgasm are part of His blueprint for marriage.

Even if you didn't grow up with mixed messages, you may still have some confusion and pain related to sex. Many couples bring sexual experiences, images, and expectations from prior relationships into marriage. When you marry, your past doesn't simply disappear. This can become problematic because our most powerful sexual organ isn't between our legs; it's our brains. The sexual images you were exposed to in previous relationships, or indirectly through pornography and other sources, can create problems in your marriage.

Can we be perfectly blunt? We don't think it's possible for a couple to experience healthy sex if one or both partners are addicted to porn. Porn is taking marriages down at a frightening rate. It's fake intimacy. That's the bad news. The good news is that when a person courageously gets help for a porn addiction, the marriage and even the sexual relationship with his or her spouse can be restored. Please don't be ignorant of the power of the mind. Your brain has a strong impact on your sex life.

If you're currently having sexual issues in your marriage, if your sexual relationship is difficult to talk about, or if one or both of you are frustrated about the frequency of sex, please be courageous enough to seek help. The sexual dimension of your marriage is too important to ignore. Don't simply hope that sexual issues will resolve themselves. They won't. Hoping that problems will go away isn't an effective strategy, and it won't lead you toward a healthy relationship. Sexual issues can become increasingly painful and drive a wedge between you and your spouse. Please know that you aren't alone in your pain. This issue is more common than you may realize. Actually, it's such a serious issue that millions of desperate couples search for answers on the Internet. In fact, a former quantitative analyst at Google who researched online search trends made this observation in the *New York Times*: "On Google, the top complaint about a marriage is not having sex. Searches for 'sexless marriage' are three and a half times more common than [searches for] 'unhappy marriage.'"[6] Again, you're not alone in your pain and frustration. There's hope! Help is available.

A UNIQUE TYPE OF BONDING

When the sexual domain in your marriage is good, it sets your entire marriage up to win. Sex makes your relationship unique and different from all your other relationships. You share something with your spouse that you share with no one else.

Sex is much more powerful than having an orgasm or experiencing a feel-good moment. It's a connection that bonds you together physically, mentally, emotionally, and even spiritually. It screams, "We are one! We are united!"

Jesus said, "A man will leave his father and mother and be *united* to his wife."[7] The word *united* in the language of the Old Testament (Hebrew) means "to be bonded to one another." That type of bonding delivers results.

According to a Pew Research Center survey, a "happy sexual relationship" ranked second after marital faithfulness for 70 percent of adults, who said it was "very important" for a successful marriage.[8] Both men and women reported higher levels of overall happiness in marriage when they experienced frequent sexual activity with their spouse.[9] Those are very strong numbers you can't afford to ignore if your sexual intimacy is drifting.

NEVER STOP DEVELOPING SEXUAL INTIMACY

If you want to experience sexual intimacy in your marriage, it's essential to understand the following key principles.

Emotional intimacy precedes sexual intimacy. Without a loving, emotional connection, sex is merely a physical act that lacks the fullness intimacy has to offer. Strangers can get together and have sex, but not with the fulfillment and joy of an emotionally healthy couple. Married sex is intended to be so much more than just a physical act. I (Doug) know that when Cathy feels good about *us* and feels emotionally connected to me, it's so much easier and more pleasurable to be physically intimate.

If your spouse isn't "into you," she won't be into sex (and vice versa). If there is no time to talk, connect, and care for what personally interests your spouse, the emotional domain of the relationship will become malnourished. Bottom line: developing a deep emotional connection in your marriage is what undergirds a dynamic sexual relationship. That emotional connection—feeling loved and valued—is something you must experience daily so you don't drift emotionally.

What if you woke up tomorrow and loved your spouse as if it were your last day together? Wouldn't you feel the urgency and importance of letting your spouse know that you love him or her deeply? Why not make that a daily habit? Begin each day as if it's going to be your last, and nurture your emotional connection. Then wake up the next morning and repeat the process. When your emotional connection deepens, your physical connection will more naturally follow.

Foreplay begins before you get to the bedroom. Foreplay is much more than flirting with your spouse and gently touching the right spots immediately preceding sex. True foreplay is often about meeting *all* your spouse's needs, not just his or her physical needs. It begins with making an emotional connection from the moment you wake up in the morning. Believe it or not, sex sometimes begins in the kitchen or the garage or when you do something you know will express your love and meet your spouse's needs.

When Cathy and I (Doug) were getting premarital counseling, the counselor said, "Doug, you'll quickly realize that sex starts in the morning."

As a twenty-one-year-old overdosing on testosterone, I immediately thought, *Awesome. I think I'm going to enjoy sex in the morning and in the afternoon and in the evening.* I was so naive. I soon came to understand that the counselor wasn't being literal. While sex in the morning can be a very good thing, he was referring to the way I treated Cathy in the morning. My words, my affection, my interest, and the way I valued her in the morning would prepare the way for sex in the evening. If you limit foreplay to the few minutes preceding intercourse, you'll be missing a powerful opportunity to express your love to each other.

One of our friends told us about her romantic husband, and the story had nothing to do with flowers, chocolate, candles, music, or wine. It had to do with washing dishes. She arrived home from work totally exhausted, and when she pulled into the driveway, she switched her mental gears to the mess she had left in the kitchen the night before. As she wearily wobbled into the kitchen, she was stunned: her kitchen was sparkling clean. Her husband had come home from work early and had just finished unloading the dishwasher. Her shocked look and huge smile said everything her husband needed to hear. He was so sexy to her at that moment. Even though he had gained weight and lost hair, he never looked more desirable. He didn't come home early from work to clean the kitchen in exchange for sex; he came home early to serve his wife. But that caring action was the foreplay she needed to prepare her for sex and having quite the night with her husband.

Kissing keeps your hearts connected. It's a scientific fact that happy couples kiss more often.[10] Kissing is like throwing logs on a fire. It helps keep the relational connection alive and the physical passion burning in a marriage. Kissing fosters a sense of security and is known to produce a physiologically healthy link to happiness.[11] When you kiss your spouse, your body releases hormones and neurotransmitters in your brain that induce joy.[12] A German study even showed that married people who kiss every day may live longer.[13] How great is that? Kissing could add years to your life. Kissing can also relieve stress and reduce pain. It's fascinating what happens when you're kissing: your body relaxes, and the level of stress hormones like cortisol decreases, resulting in an overall sense of peace and calm.[14] Yes, kissing can even improve your mood. The feel-good hormones like dopamine and serotonin are released, and these natural chemicals often increase optimism and happiness.[15] Bottom line: kissing brings about a natural high. It's so basic and simple, and yet couples begin drifting when they stop kissing with meaning.

Cathy and I (Doug) have identified three distinct types of kisses. You're more than welcome to "steal" any of them and add them to your own kissing repertoire.

> **1. The "I love you" kiss.** This is the quick peck that expresses your love for your spouse. We challenge you to exchange this type of kiss daily and accompany it with the simple but powerful words "I love you."
>
> **2. The "I like you" kiss.** This type of kiss lingers a bit longer than the peck. Without getting all wet and sloppy, it sends the message, "I really like you, and I'm going to kiss you differently from the way I kiss my mom or grandma." (It would be weird if you kissed your mom like this!) I know of a wife who said to her husband, "I never doubt that you *love* me, but I often wonder if you *like* me." An "I like you" kiss removes all doubt. It's a little more intimate than a peck and reminds your spouse that you really do like him or her.

3. **The "I want you" kiss.** This is the most intimate and passionate of kisses. Some people have called it the "soul kiss."[16] Many would call it the "French kiss," which may date back to the early 1900s when American tourists noticed the way French women kissed.[17] This type of kiss can send the message, "Because I love you and *really* like you, I'm letting you know that *I want you* too!"

You don't have to adopt our kissing definitions, but we encourage you to make sure you don't drift from kissing your spouse on a daily basis. If you've already slowed down in the kissing department, this can be a fun habit to reintroduce in your marriage. Kissing will lead to a stronger emotional connection, deeper love and affection, increased happiness, and enriched communication, and it will make a definite difference in your sex life.

DIFFERENT SEXUAL TEMPERATURES

Even in the best of marriages, there is often a "desire gap" where one spouse has a different sexual temperature than the other spouse. If you've discovered that you and your spouse have like-minded libidos with similar sexual needs, consider yourself blessed. That's typically not the norm. It's much more likely that one of you has a stronger sexual desire, which can lead to frustration and a simmering, long-term tension in your marriage.

Before you read any further, we want to stress that we're not advocating that one of you should want more or less sex than the other. The best thing you can do for the long-term health of your marriage is understand the sexual needs and desires of your spouse and learn how to meet those needs, even if they're different from yours. If you're the one with the stronger desire for sex, you need to understand that your spouse is most likely not antisex; he or she just has less interest in it than you do. Your spouse isn't trying to hurt you, reject you, or anger you, but the simple truth is that he or she doesn't think about sex as much or want it like you do.

Cathy and I (Doug) have a desire gap in our relationship, and as the spouse with the stronger sex drive, I know how frustrating it can be when your spouse isn't interested. It feels so personal. "Why not? Why wouldn't you want to? What's wrong with you? What's wrong with me?" It can feel like rejection, yet the reality is that Cathy is in no way rejecting me. She could be loving me fully in the moment, but she's just not thinking about expressing her love for me in a sexual way. At the same time, I'm thinking, *What else is there to think about?*

Our desires are simply different, and it took years for Cathy to better understand (as the spouse with the lower sex need) that for me, sex isn't purely about pleasure or orgasm; it's also about physical and emotional intimacy, affection, and a feeling that the person who loves me the most also *wants* me. In counseling or marriage seminars, I'll often tell the lower-sex-need spouse that his or her partner probably isn't just a horny human in pursuit of an orgasm. Think about it: your spouse doesn't actually need you to have an orgasm. But he or she *does* need you and want you for connection.

Feeling wanted and connected are biggies for both of you, regardless of your sexual temperature. The spouse with the lower sexual temperature often needs to feel connected *before* sex. As we noted earlier, emotional intimacy precedes physical intimacy. Here's the irony: the spouse with the higher sexual temperature often feels most connected *after* sex. Can you see how these differences might lead to problems? If you need to feel a strong connection *before* sex and you're married to someone who feels that connection more strongly *after* sex, that increases the potential for a sexual stalemate.

Here's where we find a lot of young couples experiencing difficulty: the spouse with the higher sexual temperature gets a wounded heart when his or her spouse indicates a lack of interest in sex. The spouse with the stronger need for sex feels rejected. When the heart is hurt, the response is often *emotional distance*. If the spouse with the stronger need pulls away emotionally, it can cause his or her partner to be even less interested in sex. This negative cycle can repeat over and over.

If you're the spouse with the lower sexual temperature, once you start paying more attention to your sexual relationship and refrain from labeling your spouse as "too horny," you'll likely find him or her becoming more emotionally engaged with you. Your spouse has probably figured out that sex isn't going to happen every day of your marriage, but he or she wants sex to at least be on your mental radar. Your spouse wants to know that your sexual desire hasn't completely dried up for the week (or the month). When your spouse senses that you're interested and open, he or she may be kinder, more understanding, more attentive, and more loving toward you. When your spouse realizes that you're paying more attention to the sexual sphere of your marriage, that you're moving in your spouse's direction, and that you're making an effort to speak his or her language, there's a strong possibility that you'll see dramatic results in your relationship.

Author and sex therapist Michele Weiner Davis (unfortunate middle name for a sex therapist!) wisely wrote,

> It's a simple law of human nature. When you show your caring to your more highly sexed spouse by making sex a bigger priority in your marriage, [he or she] will appreciate your efforts and become more caring toward you. You will see it in his or her eyes. You'll start getting love notes and witness[ing] random acts of kindness. Your spouse will begin to open up and be decidedly more interested in you as a person.... It will take you back to the times in your relationship when everything was clicking.[18]

Being more responsive to your spouse's sexual needs may not produce the instant results you're craving, but you'll never know until you begin moving in his or her direction.

The key to bridging the desire gap is learning to better understand each other's needs and desires. Even though Cathy and I (Doug) still have a desire gap in our sexual relationship after thirty-plus years of marriage, I would confidently say that our sex life is healthy and even thriving because both of us have committed to understanding each other better and then selflessly seeking to meet one another's needs. I had to learn that Cathy isn't antisex at all; she just doesn't think about it 24-7 like I do. And she had to learn that I'm not a pervert who always wants sex; I want physical and emotional connection (just like she does), but that connection often happens *after* sex. This has been a journey for both of us as we move toward each other in a loving and forgiving way.

SEX ENHANCERS

When you devote time and energy to your sexual relationship, the payoff can be huge. During the first few years of your marriage, you're building the foundation for an intimate and romantic lifelong relationship. Here are a few more suggestions to help you course-correct if you're beginning to drift.

Change the routine. When you were first married, you might not have used the words *sex* and *routine* in the same sentence, but perhaps that has changed. While some routine can be good, it's often synonymous with *boring*. As in many areas of your marriage, you'll have to make adjustments to keep from crashing into the island of routine. Try reversing roles. If you're not normally the initiator, take the lead more often. Have an adventure—even if it's in the backyard. Change the atmosphere or setting, and look for ways to spice up your sex life.

Schedule sex. These two words seem to create a perfect oxymoron. While it may not sound very romantic or spontaneous, a scheduled sex appointment can give you both something to look forward to. We know a couple who has chosen Wednesday nights as their regular time for sex. As a result, Wednesday looks and feels very different in their house. They clean up their bedroom, the candles come out, they play romantic music, and they get the kids to bed early. The anticipation works for them. If finding time for sex isn't working for you, you might talk about scheduling a time each week to be physically intimate with your spouse. Some people may think this sounds a bit unromantic. However, for most who have it on their calendar, they would say it not only works for them, but they anticipate the date.

Change the time. Morning is good. Afternoon is good. Evening is good. Anytime can be good for sex, but if you're always having sex at the same time in the same place in the same way, well, you're too predictable, and predictability is the death of passion. It's time to shake things up and shift to a new time.

Practice and be positive. It may be difficult for you to believe, but your sex life will most likely get even better than it is right now if you'll continue practicing. Please don't give up if something isn't working right or a certain position doesn't feel good. Don't dismiss it for the remainder of your marriage. Try it again. Variety, creativity, and playfulness can become important ingredients to spice up your sexual experiences. Remember in chapter 6 how we talked about choosing to be positive? This is one of those areas where you don't want to immediately chase the negative. If it's not great right now, go positive and change it. We hear stories of couples who don't have rich and rewarding sex lives later in marriage because they tried something once or twice, didn't like it, and never attempted it again. Practice. Practice. Practice.

Don't give up. We know of women who couldn't experience orgasms during their first few years of marriage, and instead of attempting different approaches, they felt defeated and decided that they weren't capable of orgasm. If you're struggling to reach orgasm, do some research, seek out answers, and don't abandon the journey. If only one of you is experiencing orgasm, your lack of pleasure will take its toll on your sex life. Multiple studies show that many women have difficulty reaching orgasm if they have only vaginal inter-course.[19] If orgasm doesn't come easy to you, please know you're not alone. The majority of research has emphasized the importance of clitoral stimulation for women to experience climax.[20] The more you experiment, make each other feel safe with your bodies, and accept each other, the more satisfying the sexual arena of your marriage will be. Please, please, please, don't concede too soon and think it won't be *that* big of a deal. It is a big deal! Keep experimenting until you find your way to orgasm.

Pray together. We know what you're thinking: *Really? What does prayer have to do with sex?* Marriage experts reveal that couples who pray together actually have better sex lives. It's pretty stunning that one of the top five reported sex needs of women is *spiritual intimacy*.[21] Prayer connects us to God and to our spouses, which is why spiritually compatible couples are known to have more fre-quent and fulfilling sex. Remember what we wrote earlier in the chapter? Sex is God's idea, and it was intended to be pleasurable. He's probably more than happy to have you talk to Him about it in prayer.

Flirt more. We bet you used to be good at flirting. Most couples flirt when they first meet because it opens the door to further interac-tion. Flirting helps you win another person's attention and interest. Just because you're married doesn't mean you should stop flirting with each other. Flirting is one way to flatter your spouse and remind him or her of your loving thoughts.

We asked a group of newly married couples for their flirting ideas, and we found them to be both simple and beautiful:

- "When we're in a crowded room, he whispers something romantic to me that only I can hear."
- "He mailed a love letter to me at work."
- "She hates country music but turns it on to grab my attention and show me she's thinking of me."
- "He'll grab me from behind while I'm working in the kitchen, spin me around, and slow-dance with me."
- "She'll text me during the day and tell me she can't wait to have her way with me when I get home. It drives me crazy, and I think about her all day."
- "She'll buy my favorite candy bar and leave it on my windshield with a short love note that I'll see on my way to work. It's so simple, but it always makes me smile."

Notice that none of these ideas requires you to build a vacation home by hand or spend a lot of money. Flirting is best expressed as intentional acts of interest and romance.

Date weekly. As we've already noted in chapter 3, one of the best ways to keep your marriage on the right track is to be proactive about dating (day or night). If you want a happy marriage, having a consistent, weekly, nonnegotiable date is a major step in the right direction. (If you skipped this chapter because you were more interested in the topic of sex than dating, we totally understand—but go back and read it.) We're fully aware that this commitment can be complicated, yet the positive results of spending time together on a date are extremely beneficial for marriages. Research shows that couples who deliberately establish a regular time to connect and have fun at least once a week are approximately three and a half times more likely to report being "very happy" in their marriages than those who didn't date.[22] Plus, as we've already noted, one of the added benefits of a weekly date is the increased interest in sexual intimacy.

If your sex life isn't what you want it to be, this is the time to talk together about specific course corrections and work to fix what has caused you to drift. Even if this seems like a minor issue, please do whatever it takes to deal with it before the drift intensifies. In our (Cathy and Doug's) first year of marriage, sex wasn't that great. It would occasionally hurt Cathy, we weren't on the same page in terms of desire and frequency, and I felt as if I was always the initiator. I'm so grateful today that neither of us gave up but kept moving toward each other! Our sex life continues to get better and better with practice. When it comes to sex, the learning curve is steep, and I love that we're both committed to keep practicing.

You don't want to be the couple who didn't take action and then watched your sexual relationship morph from romantic sexual partners to nonsexual roommates. You're not the only ones who encounter problems in this area, so please don't struggle in silence and allow this very treatable issue to negatively influence your marriage. Deal with the situation now, and seek out some help if you need it!

QUESTIONS

1. If you and your spouse have drifted a bit in your physical intimacy, how comfortable do you feel talking it over with each other?
2. What do you think about the phrase "Happy sex life, happy couple"?
3. How would each of you describe your current sexual temperature as individuals?

Chapter Nine

•

ENJOY YOUR BABY

Cathy and I (Jim) struggled with infertility for a number of years, so one of the greatest moments of our lives happened when Christy Meredith Burns arrived in our home. We viewed Christy's adoption as a rich blessing from God. Filled with elation and confusion, we carried her through our front door when she was just two days old. We had no idea what we were doing as new parents. I remember changing her diaper, looking at Cathy, and saying, "What do you think we should do next?"

Ironically, three decades and three daughters later, we're still asking the same question about our beautiful, grown children. The role of parent never leaves you! When a baby arrives, you quickly realize that your life and marriage will change *forever*.

Raising children has been one of the greatest experiences of our lives, and we wouldn't trade it for anything in the world. But in the interest of full disclosure, we want you to know that when a child enters your home, it may complicate your marriage in ways you never expected. To keep the drift at bay, you'll definitely need to be intentional about energizing your marriage *while* you enjoy your baby. It can't be one or the other; it must be both! Maintaining a healthy marriage postbaby requires additional time and energy, which is exactly what you don't have once the baby arrives.

When my (Doug's) wife, Cathy, became pregnant with our first child, our friends with children seemed to be the most excited for us. But they also scared us with comments like, "You have no idea what is about to hit you in a few months." At first we rolled our eyes, but soon after the baby arrived, we realized our friends were prophets. It's an amazing fact of life that no matter how ready you think you are or how much advice you get from other parents, you really don't understand the intensity and 24-7 care that's required when you become a parent. If you're already a parent, you understand this reality, but if you aren't one yet, you'll just have to trust us when we say that your life will drastically change. You're in for a beautiful, messy, new way of doing life while navigating marriage toward your desired destination. If you're wondering what's going to change, the answer is *everything*.

GET READY, GET SET, CHANGE

First-time parents experience what is often referred to as the "baby quake," which is an allusion to the chaos an earthquake causes. Since we live in California, we know a thing or two about earthquakes, and while we can't predict them, we can prepare for the aftermath. Couples who anticipate the changes parenthood will bring and make course corrections function better as parents than those who are unprepared.

As you read this chapter, remember that we want you to win big in marriage and enjoy your baby. We don't want to discourage you in our efforts to prepare you. Instead, we want to encourage you to discuss the issues *before* they become issues. Studies reveal a decline in the overall quality of marital satisfaction, especially in the first three years after a baby is born.[1] It's not unusual for a couple to say something like, "We weren't ready for the nose-dive our marriage took after our first child was born." One parent confessed to us, "It's amazing how a twelve-to-twenty-pound human had the superpowers to turn us into resentment-filled, sleep-deprived, sexless zombies." Those who aren't parents might be laughing at that statement, but those with children are nodding in agreement. If you plan to be parents, don't be scared; just do your homework so you'll be aware. Following is a partial list of what you can expect when you have a child. (If you're already a parent, let this remind you that you're not alone.)

Sleep deprivation. You won't get enough sleep in the early months (or years), and sleep loss can make you irritable and turn relatively simple tasks into huge ordeals. Tired people have shorter fuses, which typically means relational conflict is more likely. One woman told us, "I'd never been more annoyed with my husband than after the baby was born. I kept blaming him for everything. But once I got some sleep, my energy returned, and it was like I was a new person. I wasn't annoyed as much." Being tired is synonymous with being new parents.

Doubled domestic duties. It doesn't seem plausible, but there's so much more to do when you have a child who adds to the workload and yet can't help with the chores. Diapers. Bottles. Lost pacifiers. Diapers. Laundry. Diapers. You find yourself thinking, *What did we* *do with our time before she was born?* This increased work can cause additional bickering, negativity, and resentment in your marriage.

Money stress. Babies are more expensive than couples typically plan for. The added financial stress often coincides with a reduction in work hours, and the bank account begins to atrophy. Baby "stuff" adds up, since most new parents don't want to wait to buy things for their precious newborn.

Change in focus. It's not uncommon for a nursing mom to shift her focus from her husband to the newborn. I (Doug) remember feeling like a stranger in my own home during the baby's first six months. Honestly, it was a really hard time for me. I'll admit I was being selfish, but I felt as if Cathy was giving everything to our child, and there was nothing left for me. Plus, when the baby cried because she was hungry, I wasn't too much help, since I wasn't lactating. I'd hand her off to Cathy, feel like a failure as a new dad, and experience the double sting of rejection. Cathy wasn't excluding me intentionally, but the baby couldn't take care of herself, and since I could fend for myself, Cathy directed her attention and energy to the crying baby. I should have seen this coming, because it's common for a new mom to have strong feelings for her baby, but I missed it. This type of experience day in and day out definitely wreaks havoc on a husband's psyche. Many men feel jealous, distant, and forgotten but find it difficult to express those feelings because they're afraid of sounding selfish. We think that although the husband loves the baby, he often feels resentment toward his wife because of her new focus and passion for their child.

Sex frequency decreases. As a result of everything we've discussed so far, the romantic and physical connection in a marriage takes a lower priority when a child is added to the mix, and sex can become a distant memory. In addition to fatigue, a lot is going on within the wife: hormones are a little messed up following the birth, breastfeeding can lower the female libido, and some women don't feel sexy or desirable because their bodies may have changed shapes and sizes. After you become parents, your sex life will definitely require your attention, honest conversations, and some thoughtful course corrections. The sexual disconnect doesn't have to last forever, but there will most likely be a downturn in desire and frequency of sex.

Conflict increases. You don't need to be a trained counselor to realize that any of the factors we've just listed can lead to increased conflict in your marriage. Along with the joy and rejoicing over the new baby in your life, there will also be a lot of tension from frustration, exhaustion, and unmet expectations.

We love being parents! It's one of the genuine highlights of our lives, and we hope the same is true for you. If you haven't had a baby yet, we encourage you to take advantage of sleeping in, taking long showers, going to the movies together, cuddling on the couch, walking in the moonlight, and having spontaneous sex—actually, spontaneous *anything*. Your baby won't make these activities impossible, just less frequent. Although every stage of marriage has its moments of enjoyment, make sure to really enjoy your time together before you have children so you'll have a stronger marital relationship when the kids arrive.

By now you may be thinking, *Are you guys trying to scare us into staying on birth control?* That's a fair question considering what you just read, but our answer is a strong and passionate no! What we're trying to do is prepare you for the greatest privilege of your life—being a parent—which can collide with the greatest adventure of your life—being married. This requires honestly informing you of some of the issues that will arrive with the baby, and these issues definitely aren't as cute and cuddly as a newborn. You'll do fine if you know what's coming your way, take the time to discuss these issues together, and commit to prioritizing your marriage.

One of our goals for this book is to help minimize the obscene number of divorces that occur after children arrive. Given the changes that will be required of you as new parents, let's discuss some ways you can build a stronger bond as a couple.

COMMIT TO THE RELATIONAL HIERARCHY OF HEALTH

The couples who thrive in their relationship while juggling parenthood are typically those who establish priorities for their primary relationships and responsibilities and maintain them. Here's the relational hierarchy we recommend for a healthy marriage:

> God
> Marriage
> Children
> Vocation
> Everything else

You don't want to be a couple with confused priorities. Far too many couples mix up their relational priorities and then wonder why they've experienced a marital drift. We believe that if you put your relationship with God first, emphasize your marriage next, give attention to your children after this, and then focus on work and other relationships, you'll set yourself up to win in marriage.

During the first few years of marriage, it's too easy to drift from those key priorities, and before you know it, they've been rearranged. Children and your vocation will jockey for the number-one and number-two spots because they require so much time. As a result, your intimacy with God and each other will drop in the pecking order.

Our suggestion is that you ask God to give you the love, power, strength, wisdom, and discipline to keep your priorities straight. Maintaining those priorities will require ongoing attention, frequent conversations, and constant course corrections. This is definitely a fluid process, and you'll have to keep reminding yourselves, "We put God first, our marriage second, our kids third, work fourth, and everything else last." This is the order of priorities that will keep your marriage headed in the right direction.

GET SOME REST!

This isn't as easy as it sounds for new parents, but rest has the ability to heal, soothe, and restore perspective. I (Jim) still remember the day I came home from work to find our two-year-old sitting on her potty chair fast asleep and my wife curled up in a ball asleep on the bathroom floor. It was quite the sight! Her body position screamed, "I'm exhausted." We learned that whenever our daughter napped, it was a good idea to follow suit. Don't feel guilty or think you're being lazy for resting whenever you can. You need all the rest you can get!

As a couple, you may want to develop a strategy that allows the *most* tired spouse to rest so that he or she will be *less* tired. Fatigue isn't a strong marriage posture, and it requires teamwork to find refreshment. Some couples take turns feeding the baby in the middle of the night. By alternating nights, each of them gets a little extra sleep.

As our kids got a little older, I (Jim) tried to give Cathy some rest by taking our three girls out for donuts and a stroll on the beach every Saturday morning. Cathy could do anything she wanted on those mornings, which usually meant sleeping in and pampering herself.

I (Doug) couldn't do the Saturday donut and beach adventure like Jim because we were a sports family and had different practices and games on Saturday mornings. Instead, I gave Cathy shorter breaks throughout the week after I came home from work in the early evening. She was a stay-at-home mom and was often exhausted by the time I'd walk in the door. My routine was to stop by Taco Bell on my way home and decompress for about thirty minutes with a caffeinated drink and a little mindless reading. Then I could bounce in the house and say, "Go! I got this. Sneak away and do anything you want without one of these little ones pushing, hanging, crawling, and wiping on you. Enjoy yourself. We'll all be here when you return—hopefully injury-free."

While she was tempted to leave for three days, she often took just a short thirty- to sixty-minute break, but it was amazing what that short amount of time away did for her in terms of rest and recovery. Something simple like walking with a friend, getting her nails done, or shopping by herself were all gifts that gave her renewed life and energy. This tired season of married life definitely required teamwork.

LEARN TO REFRESH YOURSELF

When we surveyed couples in their first few years of marriage, more than 50 percent admitted they did very little proactively to refresh their lives personally or as a couple. Finding time to refresh yourself isn't just a good idea; it's how God wired you. He knows what you need to live life to the fullest. The Bible says, "In six days the LORD made heavens, the earth, the sea, and everything in them; but on the seventh day he rested."[2] The Hebrew word for "refreshed" actually means "to exhale." Even God rested, took a breath, built this concept of rest and restoration into the DNA of humanity, and then required us to experience a Sabbath. *Sabbath* is the Hebrew word for "rest." With the pace of life today, you must be proactive in finding refreshment. Without it, you risk becoming overcommitted and underconnected as a couple. (Be sure to review this in chapter 4.)

Here are some practical ideas for refreshment that showed up in our survey:

- Ben and Loretta give each other a five-hour alone time once a week.
- Carly and Nathan find refreshment on their weekly date night.
- Dennis and Tanya try to watch one comedy show on television every week. Laughter is a great source of refreshment for them.

- Josh and Stacy take walks together.
- Joyce and Tanner took a massage class at a local community college and then began to practice on each other. Joyce calls it "massage night," while Tanner uses other descriptive words. (We'll leave that to your imagination.)

Here's the point: no *single way* of finding rest and refreshment works for every couple. Do whatever is necessary to give yourselves a break from the routine. Find something that not only restores you personally but also rejuvenates your relationship as a couple. Here are some more practical ideas.

Join a young couples' group. Cathy and I (Jim) joined a couples' group when our kids were very young, and it breathed life into our tired souls and bodies. Every week we were with other couples who had kids of the same age and were experiencing similar issues as parents. We laughed together, challenged one another in our marriages and our parenting, and helped replenish one another. You'll want to have some people in your life who support you and reenergize you. If you have friendships that drain you, you'll have a much more difficult time as a couple and as parents. The people you surround yourselves with can have a significant impact on your life and marriage—for good or bad.

Get out of the house. This can be with or without your child. Fresh air, fresh faces, and fresh conversation can make a fresh difference. Getting out of the house regularly and connecting with others—especially your spouse—can relieve the feelings of loneliness and isolation so many parents of young children experience. As we mentioned in chapter 3, couples who play and enjoy outdoor adventures together tend to be more closely connected than couples who don't. Experiment with various recreational activities until you find one that brings you together and gets you out of the house.

Daily couple time. It's not a great mystery that developing a strong marital relationship requires time and intimacy. A theme throughout this book is that you need to be intentional about staying connected and scheduling time together as a couple. When you were first dating, could you even have imagined that a day would come when you'd need to be deliberate about having conversations? Back then, talking, laughing, and being close came naturally and in large doses. But when marriage happens and children arrive, that time seems to disappear more quickly. We heard somewhere that the average American dog owner spends more time walking the dog each day than communicating with his or her spouse. That might be a funny statistic if it weren't so tragic.

Remember the 1 percent idea we talked about in chapter 4? A commitment to something as small as 1 percent of your day is only fourteen minutes and forty seconds (or fifteen minutes if you round up). We suggest you make it your goal that no matter what, you'll spend at least fifteen minutes of daily, uninterrupted time together. This time of connecting can defuse anger, frustration, and arguments as well as increase your emotional intimacy.

Keep in mind that your couple time doesn't always have to be intense. As much as Cathy and I (Doug) need to be disciplined and turn off the TV to connect, there are other times we need to turn on the TV to relax and enjoy some "veg" time together. It could be that watching TV while cuddling on the couch is more valuable at that moment than having a serious conversation about the budget or what needs to be fixed in the backyard. In the midst of all that's going on in your lives, sometimes the very best thing you can do is find the time to just be together.

REDEFINE ROMANCE

We already addressed the topic of sex in chapter 8, but when the baby comes, you'll most likely have to redefine *romance*. This is one of the more difficult adjustments new parents face. What was once spontaneous and carefree can become a chore or feel like an obligation after the baby arrives. To help you fight those feelings and enjoy your physical relationship more, here are three simple course corrections you can make.

1. Redefine foreplay. I (Doug) remember a romantic interlude Cathy and I had after the baby arrived that seemed to be moving toward sex but was suddenly interrupted when Cathy's breast milk started leaking. Hmm … that wasn't the intended outcome of foreplay. We had to stop so she could go pump milk, which pretty much killed the moment. We can chuckle about it now, but we weren't laughing then. Physical intimacy was different because her body was acting differently. In addition, we were both so very tired all the time, so we had to make some course corrections in our physical relationship.

If your spouse is exhausted, the kind of foreplay you've been used to may need a makeover. You might want to give your spouse some time to get out of mommy or daddy mode and move into spouse mode. It could mean drawing a bubble bath, putting on some soothing music, and leaving your spouse alone for a while. The point is that what worked in the past may not work in the future, at least immediately following the birth of a child. Plus, after a vaginal birth, doctors suggest you refrain from attempting penetration for at least six weeks. We've heard of some women who beg their doctors to tell their husbands to wait six *months*.

As with any change you experience in marriage, the changes in your physical relationship will require honest communication about feelings and expectations. The more clearly and confidently you can talk about your sexual needs, the less you'll experience a drift in your relationship.

2. Redefine the frequency of sex. After the baby arrives, the frequency of sex is typically less. For some couples it's *much* less. While fatigue and other changes are a reality after birth, you've got to remember the priorities we discussed at the beginning of the chapter: *your marriage comes before your parenting.* You wouldn't neglect your child, so don't neglect your spouse. If you're tired all the time, and there's no time or energy for a physical connection, you may have your priorities in the wrong order.

While "quickies" can be both fun and satisfying, you can't have a healthy sexual diet if quickies are the only meal. On the other hand, every sexual encounter can't be a gourmet feast either. A balanced, healthy sexual diet consists of fast food (quickies) and well-cooked gourmet meals. When you become parents, you may need to change your expectations about the frequency of sex and approach it with more lead time. For example, you might say, "How about in the next two days, we take some time for a little physical intimacy? Would that work for you?" In the midst of a busy and exhausting schedule, it's very important not to neglect each other's sexual needs.

3. Clear the calendar. If you can periodically schedule a special evening together, it can do wonders for your sexual relationship and your romantic connection. I (Jim) remember a time when our youngest daughter reached the age where we could leave her for the night with a family member. It had been quite a while since Cathy and I had been away as a couple, and we needed some extended "us" time.

Cathy showed up at my office at 5:00 p.m. with a grin on her face and said, "Let's go. I'm kidnapping you. Your appointments for tomorrow morning are all canceled, and with the help of your assistant, your calendar is 100 percent clear, which means you're all mine."

Cathy had made reservations at a local bed-and-breakfast just seven minutes from our house. Honestly, it felt a little shady checking into this place in our own city, but trust me, I got over it quickly. She had packed my clothes (which was a bit rough for me as a control freak) and thought through all the details for our little getaway. We had a great night of food, conversation, and sex. The following morning we had breakfast and took a walk, and by noon we checked out and returned to our full life with three kids and our jobs. The connection and romance that took place during those nineteen hours made a huge impact on our relationship. Cathy's thoughtfulness and willingness to take the initiative created that memory and started a kidnapping tradition in our marriage.

KEEP FIRST THINGS FIRST

The very best thing you can do for your child is continue to develop a vibrant, healthy relationship with your spouse. You may be parents, but you are first and foremost a couple. A strong marriage will give your children a sense of security and well-being. When a marriage is growing, it minimizes a child's fear of losing his or her parents to divorce. It feels counterintuitive, but the more you draw close to your spouse, the better your child will ultimately feel about life. The flip side of this is a child-focused marriage and home, which can produce entitled children who grow up thinking that life is all about them. If you want to be a good role model for your children, you must prioritize your marriage above your parenting.

Parenting is one of the most sacred privileges in life, as well as one of the most difficult. It will require teamwork and your very best efforts. We're convinced that you'll become a confident parent when you become an intentional parent.[3] Intentional parents pursue good communication in their marriage, making sure they get on the same page regarding parenting expectations, styles, discipline, and many other issues that require cooperation.

As parents, you'll have a lot to learn, so we want to challenge you to commit to read one parenting book and one marriage book each year. We also recommend seeking out an older couple as marriage and parenting mentors. It's important to find trustworthy people you can learn from who will give you sound advice. Most of all, make sure to give your marriage all the attention you possibly can. It's absolutely the best thing you can do for your marriage and your family. As we both look back, the early years of parenting are now a blur, and our kids are long past diapers and midnight feedings. Without question, those years were the best and hardest of times, but we wouldn't have traded them for the world! As you embark on this parenting journey, we offer this encouragement:

buckle your seat belt, keep your marriage destination (goal) in clear view, and enjoy the ride!

QUESTIONS

1. What major changes have you seen in your marital relationship since the baby arrived? If you don't have a child yet, what changes do you expect?
2. What can you do to give each other more rest and refreshment in the midst of meeting your child's (or children's) needs?
3. If you could request one thing from your spouse to improve romance in your marriage, what would it be?

Chapter Ten

•

KEEP YOUR PROMISE

When Cathy and I (Jim) were married one week after our college graduation (which isn't something I suggest others do), I remember my mother asking, "Are you sure you two are old enough to take on the responsibility of marriage?"

I got defensive and confidently fired back, "Of course! We're in love."

Today I laugh at my arrogance and naïveté. The truth was that we had *no idea* what we were embarking upon. Immediately after the wedding, we drove up the California coast for our honeymoon, and since we had little money, we ended up staying at my cousin's house in Lake Tahoe (which is something else I don't recommend, since it doesn't exactly say "romantic").

Let me spare you some details and just cut to the chase: since we didn't prepare well for marriage, our first year was a very rocky adjustment for both of us. We were just two kids from dysfunctional homes who brought our own wounds and flaws into our marriage.

Reflecting on our forty-plus years together, I'm absolutely convinced that the odds of us surviving our marriage were slim. We've often said that without the promise we made to each other at our wedding, our marriage wouldn't have survived. The cement that has held our marriage together all these years is our commitment to that promise and a reliance on God's love for us and His strength that has empowered us to endure.

Looking back, Doug and I realize that what has kept both of our marriages strong, secure, and safe is what we refer to as "the power of a promise." When things got tough, we didn't give up on our promise. As you read this final chapter, it's our prayer that you will not only remember the very special promise you made to your spouse on your wedding day but that it will hold new meaning for you and lead to a renewed commitment to each other.

Studies reveal that two-thirds of unhappy marriages actually become happy within five years if couples persevere.[1] Think about that: *two-thirds*! That's an amazing and hopeful statistic. The power of a promise is deeply connected to your ability to persevere.

Hopefully by this point in the book, you know you're not alone in your struggle with marriage tensions and frustrations. We also hope you've given up the illusion that you'll have a problem-free marriage. Good, strong marriages don't just happen. They're the result of realizing when you're beginning to drift, making the appropriate course corrections, and learning along the way. Pain, tensions, issues, and frustration can actually become the fertilizer for a fruitful marriage. Fertilizer stinks, but it's essential for growth and beauty and the ability to bear the type of fruit that's found in God's Word: "love, joy, peace, patience, kindness, goodness, faithfulness, gentleness, and self-control."[2] That kind of fruit doesn't grow without some adversity and God's help.

Our friend David got engaged to a wonderful woman, but he was constantly questioning the viability of their marriage because they seemed to argue more than he thought was normal. David's mentor told him, "You'll have to decide if you want to spend the rest of your life arguing with Julie or arguing with someone else. Arguments, disagreements, and tension will be part of your marriage no matter who you marry. The question is, can you see yourself loving and arguing with Julie for the rest of your life?"

The mentor's wisdom gave David the certainty he needed to move forward. Today, David and Julie are happily married with three children. David recently told us, "My mentor's advice emerges every time [Julie and I are] in an argument, and I think, *I'm so glad I'm arguing with you.*"

David knows there's no such thing as a perfect, pain-free marriage, and that reality gives him the confidence he needs to keep moving forward in the power of his promise.

YOUR WEDDING VOWS

Our assumption is that when you got married, you recited some type of vow to each other. A vow is a promise. It's a covenant or binding agreement before God, each other, family, and friends that you commit to stay together until death parts you. Divorce isn't part of this agreement.

Cathy and I (Jim) repeated vows that went something like this:

> I, Jim, take you, Cathy, to be my wife. I promise
> and covenant before God and these witnesses to
> be your loving and faithful husband in plenty and
> in want, in sickness and in health, in joy and in
> sorrow, in good times and hard times, with God's
> grace and strength, as long as we both shall live.

That's a pretty incredible profession for two people to make to each other. Does it remind you of the promise you made on that very special day? Let's break it down.

I take you to be my wife/husband. Out of more than seven billion people on this planet, you chose your spouse. That choice was intended to change your life. You made a conscious decision to leave your parents and be joined with another person—"a man will leave his father and mother and be united to his wife."[3] You determined to forgo all the other options out there—ex-boyfriends or girlfriends, people you knew, those you hoped to know, those you saw online or on a dating app—and you decided to use these words: "I choose you." Those are powerful words. You made a choice, and it was a great one.

I promise and covenant before God and these witnesses. You and your spouse promised before God, the creator of all things (including marriage), and those in attendance at your wedding that you were making a lifelong covenant commitment to each other. Your promise wasn't just a statement you said to get to the cake, the dancing, and the wedding night. Those tender and truthful words were a guarantee that you would keep your promise.

To be your loving and faithful husband/wife. With this sentence, you promised love, fidelity, and continued loyalty. Both of these actions (love and faithfulness) give you and your spouse a strong sense of security that allows your marriage to thrive because you trust that this promise is true.

In plenty and in want. You promised that your commitment to each other isn't about money. You made a pledge to stay together, regardless of whether you live in a palace or a shack. No matter what economic situation you find yourselves in, you're not going to leave each other.

In sickness and in health. Healthy couples rarely have any idea what a vow could entail. It's much more than sticking by your spouse when he or she has a bad case of the flu or a rough menstrual cycle. You promised to stay strong regardless of health. We have a good friend whose husband became a quadriplegic four years after they were married, and she lives out this promise every day. When we asked her, "How do you manage?" she said, "No one said marriage would be uncomplicated. But I've found a deeper joy and love than I could have ever imagined in sticking by my husband through this trauma. That doesn't mean it has been easy, and there are days I beg God for strength just to make it through, but I made this promise when he was healthy, and I'm going to honor that vow while he's sick." Her words beautifully express the power of this promise.

In joy and in sorrow. We've experienced some of our closest moments with our spouses during intense times of sorrow over the loss of a loved one, deep disappointment with friends and family, or hurt and disappointment with each other. During difficult times, you either draw together or you drift further apart. The power of the promise is intended to minimize the drift.

In good times and hard times. Celebration comes from the good times, and relational depth and intimacy are often found in surviving the hard times. When our (Cathy and Jim's) daughter Heidi was born with a major heart complication, a social worker with poor bedside etiquette entered the hospital room and told us, "Eighty-five percent of people in your situation wind up getting a divorce." While we weren't exactly thinking about the health of our marriage at that moment, I do remember flying in an air ambulance from Orange County, California, to Boston, Massachusetts, with our five-day-old daughter, who was facing open-heart surgery. I recall looking at Cathy and thinking, *I don't know what's going to happen with Heidi, but what I do know is that we aren't going to add to that divorce statistic.* I had confidence at that moment because I had confidence in the promise I made to my wife. Being a faithful husband or wife in good times and hard times is literally an act of the will.

With God's grace and strength. Doug and I have been involved in counseling hundreds of couples, and we've never heard any of them say they regretted drawing upon the grace and strength of God for help in their marriages. On the other hand, almost daily we hear terrible stories of broken marriages in which couples tried to draw strength from different sources. *Grace* is the biblical promise of God's love for you even though you don't deserve it. His love is freely given. *Strength* is an ordinary word, but what makes it extraordinary and life changing is when you tap into God's power for your life. When you do, you have access to His unlimited resources.

Every couple makes their own faith choices. We can't force our faith on you (and that's not our style anyway), but before you finish this book, we want to encourage you to put your faith in Jesus and His promises in the Bible, follow Him, align your lives with His teachings, and become a couple who says, "As for me and my house, we will serve the LORD."[4]

As long as we both shall live. These words take the marriage covenant to the very edge of eternity. As long as you're breathing, the commitment you made to your spouse is in effect. This promise of staying together until someone dies provides the hope marriages need during troubled seasons, as well as feelings of joy and celebration during the good times. When you know you're committed to each other for life, it changes everything.

Our guess is that you were a lot like us on your wedding day and really didn't have a clear idea what your promise would entail. But the magnitude of that promise hit home during your first few years of marriage. By revisiting and reviewing your wedding vows, you'll minimize the drift and maximize your love for each other. Your marriage is intended to last, and you made a promise that will have a ripple effect for your children and grandchildren. Your legacy will inspire future generations. We want to challenge you to keep your promise.

COMPLETE DEVOTION

We know of a woman who was married for a few years, had two children, and became busy with work and kids. She admitted to neglecting her marriage and allowing it to drift from its intended destination. As a result of the drift, she made some poor choices and ended up having an affair with a coworker. It was very exciting to her—the clandestine meetings, the unbridled passion, the urgency to reconnect, the physical ecstasy she wasn't experiencing in her marriage, and the mystery of what could be. All of this added up to a choice to walk away from her marriage. But like so many stories we've heard before, her affair soon followed the path of most. It gradually became predictable and routine—and it, too, experienced the drift. The affair that destroyed her marriage and cost her the respect of her husband, children, and family didn't last.

At her parents' fiftieth wedding anniversary, the entire family gathered to celebrate this incredible milestone. She found herself caught between joy for her parents and guilt over her own situation. She sat alone in the background, watching all the fun and laughter, thinking to herself, *What helped my parents make it to fifty years?* She knew their marriage didn't lack passion, but she also knew they didn't experience the physical ecstasy she'd had with her ex-lover. What was it about her parents' love that made the difference? The answer slowly dawned on her: Their legacy of love resulted from the power of the promise they made fifty years ago. They made a vow to each other on their wedding day, and they recommitted to it daily. Her mom and dad had what she now craved. She saw firsthand the power of a fifty-year promise.

At a recent marriage conference, we noticed an elderly couple entering with the help of their walkers. We smiled and quickly made our way over to greet them. I (Jim) asked them how long they'd been married. They took each other's hands, and she proudly said, "Sixty-six years."

I (Doug) then asked, "Why did you come to a marriage conference? You should be the ones giving out advice."

They looked at each other, and he said, "We can always learn something to help us love each other more."

The cute elderly wife nodded in agreement.

I (Jim) said, "Please give us your secret to the longevity and the strength of your marriage."

They looked at each other again and smiled, and then the husband said, "We made a commitment to always pursue each other, and we've never stopped."

This committed couple taught an entire marriage seminar in that one sweet and powerful statement. We were deeply moved by their words and actions.

What we observed in that older couple was a depth of love that seemed to defy the *dictionary* definition. In the English language, we have just one word for love, while both the Hebrew and the Greek have several different words. The word most often used in the Old Testament for the love of a married couple is *ahava*. For the Hebrews, *ahava* wasn't an emotion; it was an action. The closest phrase we have in English might be "complete devotion." *Ahava* means being faithful to the end, or completely devoted. That sweet couple of sixty-six years probably had never heard of *ahava*, but they were definitely modeling it in their love for each other.

I remember a time when Cathy and I (Jim) were in one of those rough spots in our relationship. It was an evening I'll never forget because the tension was unusually high. The irony is that I don't even remember what our fight was about, but I do remember my feelings. Cathy said something that triggered a fear, and I shot back with a nasty comment, and it was game on. We said some awful things to each other. Back then, our poor style of conflict management meant that she wanted to fight and I wanted to flee. Each of us said just enough to hurt the other person, and then we wisely decided to take a break and go our separate ways in the house.

Later that evening when we came back together, I said to her, "I don't know what happened earlier. I do know both of us have some fault in it, but I want you to know I'm not going anywhere."

Cathy received those words and repeated them: "Good! Because I'm not going anywhere either."

That simple declaration became a powerful moment for us. Those were words of *ahava*.[5] By the way, Jesus shows *ahava* love for you. You mess up and have sin in your life because you're not perfect. In spite of that, He shows you *ahava* love. He stays. He pursues you. He believes in you. No matter how messy your life gets, He isn't going away or leaving you. He is completely devoted to you.

AHAVA ON DISPLAY

Like God's love for you, not giving up on your spouse or bailing when it's tough is one of the most heroic actions you can take. Robertson McQuilkin most likely never realized that what he did for his wife would one day be called heroic. Robertson was the president of Columbia International University in South Carolina. After he and his wife, Muriel, had been married more than forty years, she developed Alzheimer's disease. Robertson found himself caught between two divine callings. One was the promise and commitment he made to his wife in sickness and in health, and the other was his commitment to the university he loved. He could easily have gotten help for his wife so he could carry on his important responsibilities at the school he was leading so effectively. But instead of continuing to work, Robertson McQuilkin resigned from his prestigious role to care for his wife full-time. Here is part of his resignation speech, which reveals *ahava*, or complete devotion:

> I haven't in my life experienced easy decision making on major decisions. But one of the simplest and clearest decisions I've had to make is this one, because circumstances dictated it. Muriel, now in the last couple of months, seems to be almost happy when with me, and almost never happy when not with me. In fact, she seems to feel trapped, becomes very fearful, sometimes almost terror[ized], and when she can't get to me, there can be anger.... She's in distress. But when I'm with her, she's happy and contented. And so I must be with her at all times, and you see, it's not only that I promised in sickness and in health, till death do us part, and I'm a man of my word, but I have said ... publicly, it's the only fair thing. She sacrificed for me for forty years to make my life possible. So if I cared for her for forty years, I'd

still be in debt. However, there's much more. It's
not that I have to; it's that I get to. I love her very
dearly.... She's a delight, and it's a great honor to
care for such a wonderful person.[6]

Robertson's resignation speech is a beautiful example of following through on his wedding-day promise.

Are you ready to continue in your marriage journey with *ahava*
toward your spouse? The only way to come close to understanding
ahava is to better understand God's promise to you. God said, "I
will never leave you or forsake you."[7] In other words, "I will walk
through it all with you." Jesus died on the cross as the ultimate act
of love. In agony, He looked down at those who had denied Him,
abandoned Him, and betrayed Him, and He stayed on that cross so
that you could have an abundant life—a better life than you could
ever have in your own power.

The greatest display of love in human history is that *Jesus
stayed*. He loved you not because you were lovely but to *make* you
lovely. He stayed with you through it all. He made a promise, and
He stayed. He modeled what you're called to do in marriage. You
made a promise to your spouse, and that promise says, "I'm not
going anywhere!"

As you close this book and begin to apply some of what you've
learned, be sure to remind your spouse of your *ahava* love: "I'm not
going anywhere, I'm on this journey with you."

QUESTIONS

1. Why do you think there's such power in the promise "as long as we both shall live"?
2. *Ahava* means "complete devotion" and is more focused on action than emotion. How can an *ahava* love strengthen the foundation of your relationship?
3. Set a time to review and renew your marriage vows, and/or write your spouse a letter about what your promise means to you.

NOTES

CHAPTER 1

1. Data from National Survey of Families and Households (NSFH), analyzed in Linda J. Waite et al., *Does Divorce Make People Happy? Findings from a Study of Unhappy Marriages* (New York: Institute for American Values, 2002), 5, 33.

CHAPTER 2

1. Data from National Survey of Families and Households (NSFH), analyzed in Linda J. Waite et al., *Does Divorce Make People Happy? Findings from a Study of Unhappy Marriages* (New York: Institute for American Values, 2002), 5, 33.

2. Multiple studies cited in Dr. Les Parrott and Dr. Leslie Parrott, *Making Happy: The Art and Science of a Happy Marriage* (Brentwood, TN: Worthy, 2014), 30–33. The happiness pie diagram was published in Sonya Lyubomirsky, Kennon M. Sheldon, and David Schkade, "Pursuing Happiness: The Architecture of Sustainable Change," *Review of General Psychology* 9, no. 2 (2005): 116.

3. Cited in Dr. Greg Smalley and Erin Smalley, eds., *Ready to Wed: 12 Ways to Start a Marriage You'll Love* (Carol Stream, IL: Tyndale House, 2015), 123.

4. Matthew 7:3–5.

5. See John 15:13.

6. Ephesians 5:21.

7. Sue Johnston, quoted in J. A. Medders, *Gospel Formed: Living a Grace-Addicted, Truth-Filled, Jesus-Exalting Life* (Grand Rapids: Kregel, 2014), 118–19. Originally appeared in Hayley Hudson, "Valentine's Gesture from Dead Husband to Wife Will Make You Melt," *Huffington Post*, February 10, 2013. www.huffingtonpost.com/2013/02/10/dead-husband-valentine_n_2654726.html

CHAPTER 3

1. Proverbs 17:22 NLT.

2. Jim Burns, *10 Building Blocks for a Solid Family* (Ventura, CA: Regal, 2010), chap. 7.

3. Leonard Sweet, *SoulSalsa: 17 Surprising Steps for Godly Living in the 21st Century* (Grand Rapids: Zondervan, 2000), 158.

4. Research cited in W. Bradford Wilcox and Jeffrey Dew, *The Date Night Opportunity: What Does Couple Time Tell Us about the Potential Value of Date Nights?* (Charlottesville, VA: National Marriage Project, 2012), 3–5.

CHAPTER 4

1. Max Lucado, *God Came Near* (Nashville: Thomas Nelson, 2004), 138–39.

2. John 10:10.

3. Sally Andrews et al., "Beyond Self-Report: Tools to Compare Estimated and Real-World Smartphone Use," *PLOS One* 10, no. 10 (2015), http://journals.plos.org/plosone/article/file?id=10.1371/journal.pone.0139004&type =printable.

4. See Luke 10:38–42.

CHAPTER 5

1. Ephesians 5:33.

2. Dr. Emerson Eggerichs, *Love and Respect: The Love She Most Desires; the Respect He Desperately Needs* (Nashville: Thomas Nelson, 2004), 16.

3. Dr. Gary Chapman, *The 5 Love Languages: The Secret to Love That Lasts* (Chicago: Northfield, 2015), chaps. 4–8.

4. For more information on the love languages, or to take a short discovery test, visit www.lovelanguages.com.

5. David Olson, Amy Olson-Sigg, and Peter J. Larson, *The Couple Checkup: Find Your Relationship Strengths* (Nashville: Thomas Nelson, 2008), 128.

CHAPTER 6

1. John M. Gottman and Nan Silver, *The Seven Principles for Making Marriage Work: A Practical Guide from the Country's Foremost Relationship Expert* (New York: Harmony Books, 2015), 71.

2. Dr. Neil Clark Warren, with Ken Abraham, *Falling in Love for All the Right Reasons: How to Find Your Soul Mate* (New York: Time Warner, 2005), 35.

3. Richard B. Miller, "Marital Quality and Health over 20 Years: A Growth Curve Analysis," *Journal of Marriage and Family* 75, no. 3 (June 2013): 667–80.

CHAPTER 7

1. Denis de Rougemont, quoted in Timothy Keller, with Kathy Keller, *The Meaning of Marriage: Facing the Complexities of Commitment with the Wisdom of God* (New York: Penguin, 2011), 35.

2. John M. Gottman and Nan Silver, *The Seven Principles for Making Marriage Work: A Practical Guide from the Country's Foremost Relationship Expert* (New York: Harmony Books, 2015), 51.

3. Adapted from Michael and Amy Smalley, "Why Good Marriages Go Bad," topic 2 in *Engaged 2.0: The 8 Fundamental Truths to Lasting Love; The Training Manual* (Woodlands, TX: Smalley Impact, 2008), 34, http://smalley.cc/images/Core-Fears-Example.pdf.

4. We have titled this the "Fear Chase," but a similar type of cycle shows up in several different sources. The authors are indebted to the National Institute of Marriage and Ted Cunningham and Gary Smalley, who wrote about this in *From Anger to Intimacy: How Forgiveness Can Transform Your Marriage* (Grand Rapids: Revell, 2009), and Ted Lowe, who has a similar cycle in his book titled *Your Best Us: Marriage Is Easier Than You Think* (Cumming, GA: Orange, 2016).

5. Adapted from Smalley, "Why Good Marriages Go Bad," 33.

6. Adapted from Smalley, "Why Good Marriages Go Bad," 33.

7. Adapted from Ted Lowe, *Your Best Us: Marriage Is Easier Than You Think* (Cumming, GA: Orange, 2016).

8. William Faulkner, *Requiem for a Nun* (New York: Vintage, 1979), 73.

9. See Matthew 18:21–22.

10. See John 8:1–11.

CHAPTER 8

1. See, for example, I. Schneiderman et al., "Oxytocin during the Initial Stages of Romantic Attachment: Relations to Couples' Interactive Reciprocity," *Psychoneuroendocrinology* 37, no. 8 (August 2012): 1277–85, www.ncbi.nlm.nih.gov/pubmed/22281209.

2. Dr. Kevin Leman, *Sheet Music: Uncovering the Secrets of Sexual Intimacy in Marriage* (Carol Stream, IL: Tyndale, 2008), 4.

3. David Olson, Amy Olson-Sigg, and Peter J. Larson, *The Couple Checkup: Find Your Relationship Strengths* (Nashville: Thomas Nelson, 2008), 105–6.

4. Matt Chandler, *The Mingling of Souls: God's Design for Love, Marriage, Sex, and Redemption* (Colorado Springs: David C Cook, 2015), 11.

5. Frederick Buechner, *Beyond Words: Daily Readings in the ABC's of Faith* (San Francisco: HarperSanFrancisco, 2004), 365.

6. Seth Stephens-Davidowitz, "Searching for Sex," Sunday Review, *New York Times*, January 24, 2015, www.nytimes.com/2015/01/25/opinion/sunday /seth-stephens-davidowitz-searching-for-sex.html?_r=0.

7. Matthew 19:5.

8. "Modern Marriage," Social and Demographic Trends, Pew Research Center, July 18, 2007, www.pewsocialtrends.org/2007/07/18/modern-marriage/.

9. Edward O. Laumann et al., *The Social Organization of Sexuality: Sexual Practices in the United States* (Chicago: University of Chicago Press, 2000), 130, tables 3A and 3B; 358, table 10.4.

10. Rafael Wlodarski and Robin I. M. Dunbar, "Examining the Possible Functions of Kissing in Romantic Relationships," *Archives of Sexual Behavior* 42, no. 8, (2013): 1415–23, www.ncbi.nlm.nih.gov/pmc/articles/PMC4487821/. See also Sheril Kirshenbaum, *The Science of Kissing: What Our Lips Are Telling Us* (New York: Hachette, 2011), 101, 181–82.

11. Kirshenbaum, *Science of Kissing*, 206.

12. Kirshenbaum, *Science of Kissing*, 83, 122–23.

13. Kirshenbaum, *Science of Kissing*, 147.

14. Kirshenbaum, *Science of Kissing*, 122, 198.

15. Kirshenbaum, *Science of Kissing*, 83.

16. Kirshenbaum, *Science of Kissing*, 63.

17. Kirshenbaum, *Science of Kissing*, 62.

18. Michele Weiner Davis, *The Sex-Starved Marriage: Boosting Your Marriage Libido* (New York: Simon and Schuster, 2003), 11.

19. Elisabeth A. Lloyd, *The Case of the Female Orgasm: Bias in the Science of Evolution* (Cambridge, MA: Harvard University Press, 2005), 36.

20. Lloyd, *The Case of the Female Orgasm*, 22, 26.

21. See Dr. Gary Rosberg and Barbara Rosberg, *The 5 Sex Needs of Men & Women* (Carol Stream, IL: Tyndale, 2006), 40.

22. Survey of Marital Generosity, cited in W. Bradford Wilcox and Jeffrey
    Dew, *The Date Night Opportunity: What Does Couple Time Tell Us about
    the Potential Value of Date Nights?* (Charlottesville, VA: National Marriage
    Project, 2012), 5, http://nationalmarriageproject.org/wp-content
    /uploads/2012/05/NMP-DateNight.pdf.

CHAPTER 9

1. John M. Gottman and Julie Schwartz Gottman, *And Baby Makes Three: The
   Six-Step Plan for Preserving Marital Intimacy and Rekindling Romance after Baby
   Arrives* (New York: Three Rivers Press, 2007), 5–10, 16.

2. Exodus 20:11 NLT.

3. Two of our books may help you: Jim Burns, *Confident Parenting* (Bloomington,
   MN: Bethany House, 2007); and Doug Fields and Cathy Fields, *Intentional
   Parenting: 10 Ways to Be an Exceptional Parent in a Quick-Fix World*
   (Vancouver, WA: Kitchen Table Academy, 2015). Both of these resources are
   available at www.homeword.com/store.

CHAPTER 10

1. Data from National Survey of Families and Households (NSFH), analyzed in
   Linda J. Waite et al., *Does Divorce Make People Happy? Findings from a Study of
   Unhappy Marriages* (New York: Institute for American Values, 2002), 5, 33.

2. Galatians 5:22–23 NLT.

3. Matthew 19:5.

4. Joshua 24:15 ESV.

5. As powerful as the word and theme of *ahava* are, if there is domestic abuse
   and violence in your home, we suggest you get the help you need to discern
   whether you should stay or leave.

6. "Robertson McQuilkin's Resignation Speech," YouTube video, 1:48, posted by
   Trinity Church, Redlands, CA, February 10, 2014, www.youtube.com
   /watch?v=MqtG-XfxMC4&feature=youtu.be. See also Sarah Eekhoff Zylstra,

"Died: Robertson McQuilkin, College President Praised for Alzheimer's Resignation," *Christianity Today*, June 2, 2016, www.christianitytoday. com/gleanings/2016/june/died-robertson-mcquilkin-columbia-president-alzheimers-ciu.html.

7. Several Scripture references contain the promise that God will never forsake or abandon us: Deuteronomy 31:6, 8; Joshua 1:5; 1 Kings 8:57; 1 Chronicles 28:20; Psalm 37:28; 94:14; Isaiah 41:17; 42:16; and Hebrews 13:5.

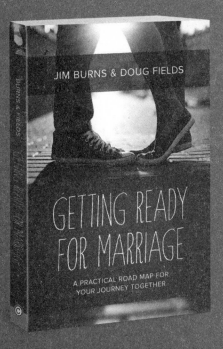

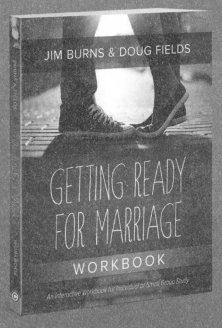